REGENTS RENAISSANCE DRAMA SERIES

General Editor: Cyrus Hoy
Advisory Editor: G. E. Bentley

GORBODUC
OR
FERREX AND PORREX

THOMAS SACKVILLE
and
THOMAS NORTON

Gorboduc
or
Ferrex and Porrex

Edited by

IRBY B. CAUTHEN, JR.

UNIVERSITY OF NEBRASKA PRESS · LINCOLN

Publishers on the Plains

UNP

Copyright © 1970 by the University of Nebraska Press
All Rights Reserved
Standard Book Number: 8032-0288-1
Library of Congress Catalog Card Number: 74-88095

MANUFACTURED IN THE UNITED STATES OF AMERICA

Regents Renaissance Drama Series

The purpose of the Regents Renaissance Drama Series is to provide soundly edited texts, in modern spelling, of the more significant plays of the Elizabethan, Jacobean, and Caroline theater. Each text in the series is based on a fresh collation of all sixteenth- and seventeenth-century editions. The textual notes, which appear above the line at the bottom of each page, record all substantive departures from the edition used as the copy-text. Variant substantive readings among sixteenth- and seventeenth-century editions are listed there as well. In cases where two or more of the old editions present widely divergent readings, a list of substantive variants in editions through the seventeenth century is given in an appendix. Editions after 1700 are referred to in the textual notes only when an emendation originating in some one of them is received into the text. Variants of accidentals (spelling, punctuation, capitalization) are not recorded in the notes. Contracted forms of characters' names are silently expanded in speech prefixes and stage directions, and, in the case of speech prefixes, are regularized. Additions to the stage directions of the copy-text are enclosed in brackets. Stage directions such as "within" or "aside" are enclosed in parentheses when they occur in the copy-text.

Spelling has been modernized along consciously conservative lines. "Murther" has become "murder," and "burthen," "burden," but within the limits of a modernized text, and with the following exceptions, the linguistic quality of the original has been carefully preserved. The variety of contracted forms (*'em, 'am, 'm, 'um, 'hem*) used in the drama of the period for the pronoun *them* are here regularly given as *'em*, and the alternation between *a'th'* and *o'th'* (for *on* or *of the*) is regularly reproduced as *o'th'*. The copy-text distinction between preterite endings in -*d* and -*ed* is preserved except where the elision of *e* occurs in the penultimate syllable; in such cases, the final syllable is contracted. Thus, where the old editions read "threat'ned," those of the present series read "threaten'd." Where, in the old editions, a contracted preterite in -*y'd* would yield -*i'd* in modern spelling (as in "try'd," "cry'd," "deny'd"), the word is here given in its full form (e.g., "tried," "cried," "denied").

Punctuation has been brought into accord with modern practices. The effort here has been to achieve a balance between the generally light pointing of the old editions, and a system of punctuation which, without overloading the text with exclamation marks, semicolons, and dashes, will make the often loosely flowing verse (and prose) of the original syntactically intelligible to the modern reader. Dashes are regularly used only to indicate interrupted speeches, or shifts of address within a single speech.

Explanatory notes, chiefly concerned with glossing obsolete words and phrases, are printed below the textual notes at the bottom of each page. References to stage directions in the notes follow the admirable system of the Revels editions, whereby stage directions are keyed, decimally, to the line of the text before or after which they occur. Thus, a note on 0.2 has reference to the second line of the stage direction at the beginning of the scene in question. A note on 115.1 has reference to the first line of the stage direction following line 115 of the text of the relevant scene.

CYRUS HOY

University of Rochester

Contents

List of Abbreviations

Cunliffe	J. W. Cunliffe. *The Influence of Seneca on Elizabethan Tragedy*. London, 1893.
Dodsley	Robert Dodsley, ed. *Old Plays*. Vol. II. London, 1744.
Fox	W. S. Fox. *The Mythology of All Races: Greek and Roman*. Boston, 1916.
Geoffrey of Monmouth	Geoffrey of Monmouth. *Histories of the Kings of Britain* (translated by Sebastian Evans). London, 1934.
Hawkins	Thomas Hawkins, ed. *The Origin of the English Drama*. London, 1773.
Herrick	M. T. Herrick. "Senecan Influence in *Gorboduc*." *Studies in Speech and Drama*. Ithaca, 1944.
Manly	John Matthews Manly, ed. *Specimens of the Pre-Shakespearean Drama*. Vol. II. Boston, 1897.
Nares	Robert Nares. *A Glossary or Collection of Words* . . . . London, 1901.
OED	*Oxford English Dictionary*
Q1	The first edition of *Gorboduc*, a quarto published in London, dated September 22, 1565.
Q2	The second edition, a quarto of 1570.
Q3	The third edition, a quarto of 1590.
Sackville-West	R. W. Sackville-West, ed. *The Works of Thomas Sackville*. London, 1859.
Scott	Walter Scott, ed. *Ancient British Drama*. Vol. I. London, 1810.
Smith	L. T. Smith, ed. *Gorboduc*. Heilbronn, 1883.

Starnes and Talbot   D. T. Starnes and E. W. Talbot. *Classical Myth and Legend in Renaissance Dictionaries.* Chapel Hill, 1955.

Swart   Jacobus Swart. *Thomas Sackville.* Groningen, 1948.

Tilley   M. P. Tilley. *A Dictionary of the Proverbs in England* . . . . Ann Arbor, 1950.

Walsh   Sister Maureen Walsh. "A Critical Edition of Gorboduc." Ph.D. dissertation, Saint Louis University, 1964.

Watt   H. A. Watt. *Gorboduc; or, Ferrex and Porrex.* Madison, 1910.

Introduction

Henry Machyn, citizen and merchant-tailor of London, noted that on December 27, 1561, there came riding through London a lord of misrule, gorgeously dressed and accompanied by a hundred horsemen with chains of gold, who rode into the Inner Temple; "for there," he writes in his diary, "was great cheer all Christmas . . . and great revels as ever for the gentlemen of the Temple every day, for many of the council were there." [1] *Gorboduc*, the "furniture of part of the grand Christmas in the Inner Temple," had been written for these great revels by two of its members—Thomas Norton, then twenty-nine, who wrote the first three acts, and Thomas Sackville, then twenty-five, who wrote the last two.[2] Norton, who was later to become known as "Rackmaster General" for his torture of Roman Catholics, and Sackville, cousin to the Queen and later her Lord High Steward, had entered the Temple some six years before. As students there, they had received training not only in liberal education and the law, but in military tactics and in music, dancing, and the drama.[3] The play,

[1] *The Diary of Henry Machyn*, ed. J. G. Nichols (London, 1848), pp. 273–274.

[2] Although some commentators like Howard Baker (*Induction to Tragedy* [Baton Rouge, 1939], p. 44) do not fully accept the title page's ascription that "three acts were written by . . . Norton, and the last two by . . . Sackville," most critics are agreed that the ascription is authentic. Not until Thomas Warton (*History of English Poetry* [1774–1781]), who assigned the whole play to Sackville, was the division of labors doubted, and modern stylistic analyses seem to bear out the attribution of authorship. The consistency of both parts is most impressive. But if Sackville wrote the last two acts to fit in with the first three, and if Norton revised Q1 for the printer of Q2 and regularized the meter, the remarkable consistency of both parts is easily explained. See Sr. Maureen Walsh, "A Critical Edition of Gorboduc" (Ph.D. diss., St. Louis University, 1964), p. 47.

[3] The Inner Temple has a distinguished connection with the literary world: along with Norton and Sackville, the Temple can boast of William Browne, Francis Beaumont, William Wycherley, James Boswell, Arthur Henry Hallam, Thomas Hughes, and Charles Lamb, and perhaps Geoffrey Chaucer as well. See A. Wigfall Green, *The Inns of Court and Early English Drama* (New Haven, 1931), pp. 3–5, 32.

designed for only one presentation on Twelfth Night, 1562, must have been a lavish production. As was customary at Christmas, the hall was strewn with rushes, and candles and torches burned in great abundance. The banquet that preceded the play was served on silverware and was accompanied by finger bowls, ewers, and rose-water basins. After the tables had been cleared, the play began on a "scaffold"[4] at the end of the hall. The actors, according to the descriptions of those in the dumb shows, must have been elaborately and gorgeously costumed. A large cast, a minimum of twenty-one, was surely required: the dumb shows require at least nine persons, perhaps more; four men are needed for the chorus; and the play itself, even if doubling were used, demands a minimum of eight players. The entr'acte music requires a new set of instruments for each act—violins, cornets, hautboys (or oboes), and drums with flutes. Economy of production was certainly not the watchword for this grand revel.[5] Such lavishness for only one production seems to have been characteristic of the Templers' entertainment. A second production, however, was royally commanded, and the play was given at Whitehall for the Queen less than two weeks later, on January 18.[6]

Queen Elizabeth was not present at the first performance, but there is no doubt that she soon heard of the play. It spoke of matters so close to her subjects' hearts—the danger of an unsettled succession to the throne—that it violated her edict (May 16, 1559) forbidding plays which touched on religion or politics, these "being no meet matters to be written or treated upon but by men of authority, learning, and wisdom, nor to be handled before any audience but of grave and discreet persons." Not just for the hearing of the grave

[4] The word is ambiguous and could mean either a stage or a raised dais for the audience. See Glynne Wickham, *Early English Stages 1300 to 1660*, II, Part 1 (London, 1963), 183. Because the Furies in Dumb Show IV come "forth from under the stage," the scaffold here is most likely a stage.

[5] D. M. Bevington, *From "Mankind" to Marlowe* (Cambridge, Mass., 1962), pp. 36–37.

[6] Only these two performances in Great Britain have been recorded. A report of a third one, mentioned by Edmund Malone (*The Plays and Poems of William Shakespeare* [London, 1821], III, 31–32) as coming from "Chatwood the prompter" and taking place at Dublin Castle in 1601, is of doubtful authenticity. However, Professor Ernest W. Talbert has privately informed me that on February 29, 1949, the Playmakers of the University of North Carolina performed a slightly abridged version of the play. I can find no other records of its performance.

subject matter discussed by young law students but, one suspects, for the satisfaction of her own royal curiosity, Elizabeth commanded that second performance at Whitehall. Machyn wrote that on "the eighteenth day of January was a play in the Queen's hall at Westminster by the gentlemen of the Temple, and after a great masque, for there was a great scaffold in the hall, with great triumph as has been seen; and the morrow after the scaffold was taken down."

Elizabeth need not have feared that these "meet matters" had been indecorously handled. The moral of the play is explicit—that for the safety of the realm there be "certain heirs appointed to the crown,/ To stay the title of established right,/ And in the people plant obedience...." But the moral, explicit as it is, is not specifically applied to the Queen. The caution that marks *Gorboduc* is lost a few years later in a play such as *A Debate on Marriage* (1565) where the participants are Juno and Diana. In this play Jupiter resolves a debate between marriage and chastity, both sides being represented by the gentlemen of Gray's Inn. At its conclusion Elizabeth is said to have remarked, "This is all against me." *Gorboduc*, so far as we know, did not inspire such a personal response openly given. We shall return to the political import of the play, but first let us look at its dramatic importance.

THE PLAY

Gorboduc is a landmark in English drama. It is the first real English tragedy; although it adheres to the Senecan tradition, it modifies that tradition in order to express certain concepts of Tudor political theory. It is the first English drama to use blank verse, afterwards the standard measure for stately matters, but then only recently introduced into England by Henry Howard, Earl of Surrey, in his translation of parts of Virgil's *Aeneid* (1554).[7] It is the first English play to use dumb shows. Moreover, it is the subject of some of the first English dramatic criticism: Sidney, in his *Defense of Poesy*, found the play "full of stately speeches and well-sounding phrases, climbing

[7] Blank verse had also been used by Nicholas Grimald in two short poems in Tottel's *Miscellany* (1557) and by Norton himself, following Surrey's lead, in translating into English some quotations from Virgil in Calvin's *Institutes*. See Howard Baker, "Some Blank Verse Written by Thomas Norton before *Gorboduc*," *Modern Language Notes*, XLVIII (1933), 529–530.

to the height of Seneca's style, and as full of notable morality." Yet for him it could not be "an exact model" of all tragedies:

> For it is faulty both in place and time, the two necessary companions of all corporeal actions. For where the stage should always represent but one place, and the uttermost time presupposed in it should be, both by Aristotle's precept and common reason, but one day, there is both many days and many places inartificially imagined.

Sidney saw the play's weakness in its ignoring of the classical unities of time and of place. Yet because of the unity of "fable," the plot, and the attempts to keep the play largely in one locale—Gorboduc's palace—as well as the five-act structure, the use of a messenger, and the banning of violence from the stage, the play has been classified as a regular tragedy, that is, one that follows the classical rules. Finally, *Gorboduc* begins the line of modern history plays; based on English history, it anticipates those later to be written by Shakespeare, Marlowe, and the lesser Elizabethans.[8] For the first time in the history of English drama, the destiny of England becomes a burning dramatic concern. Some of these and other aspects of the play deserve further consideration: its source, its use of the Senecan tradition and of a native English dramatic tradition, its Elizabethan "artifice," and its political importance.

The play is ultimately based on the story of Gorbodugo in Geoffrey of Monmouth's *Histories of the Kings of Britain* (II,xvi), and the fable of the tragedy generally follows Geoffrey's account, although other chroniclers may have been consulted:

> Unto [Gorboduc] were two sons born, whereof the one was called Ferrex and the other Porrex. But when their father began to verge upon eld, a contention arose betwixt the twain as to which should succeed him in the kingdom. Howbeit, Porrex, spurred on thereunto by a more grasping covetise, layeth snares for his brother with a design of slaying him, whereupon Ferrex, when the matter was discovered unto him, betook himself across

[8] The tragedies of *Gorboduc* and *King Lear* have some kinship, as has often been noted; for a cogent account, see B. H. Carneiro de Mendonca, "The Influence of *Gorboduc* on *King Lear*," *Shakespeare Survey 13* (Cambridge, 1960), pp. 41–48. Joan Rees (*Notes & Queries*, I [1954], 195–196) has also noticed a similarity between V.ii.213–214 in this play and *3 Henry VI*, II.v.69, "Pardon me, God, I knew not what I did."

the Channel into Gaul, and, having obtained the help of Suard, King of the Franks, returned and fought against his brother. In this battle betwixt them, Ferrex was slain together with the entire host that accompanied him. Thereupon the mother, whose name was Widen, when she learnt the certainty of her son's death, was beyond measure troubled, and conceived a bitter hatred of the other, for she loved the one that was slain better of the twain, and so hotly did her wrath blaze up by reason of his death, that she was minded to revenge it upon his brother. She accordingly took possession of the tent wherein he was lying fast asleep, and setting upon him with her waiting-women hacked him all into little pieces. Thenceforward the people was sore afflicted by civil war for a long space, and the kingdom was governed by five kings who harried the one another by mutual forays wherein was much blood spilt.[9]

The tragedy does not mention Ferrex's flight to France, and it alters the details of the slaying of Porrex by Videna, probably, as Watt has pointed out, because of the exigencies of plot. But these are but minor details: the reign of Gorboduc was seen by both the medieval and the Elizabethan as a solemn warning of what might happen to a crown and a commonwealth without the provision for an orderly succession; the horrors of civil war, the interventions of foreign power, and the injustices of despotic action were sure to follow.

The same story, emphasizing the civil wars that prey upon a leaderless land, is told by the chroniclers succeeding Geoffrey—Wace (1155), Layamon (1205), Matthew of Westminster (1327), Higden (1327), Fabyan (1516), Rastell (1529), Hardyng (1543), and Lanquet (1559). H. A. Watt believes that Grafton's version was the basis for the play, but that version had not been published when *Gorboduc* was produced.[10] Jacobus Swart chooses Fabyan as "nearest to the

[9] This is Sebastian Evans' translation in the Everyman Library edition of Geoffrey (London, 1934), pp. 35–36. Marguerite Hearsey, in her edition of Sackville's *Complaint of Buckingham* (New Haven, 1936), suggests that he came upon the story of Gorboduc while he was unearthing materials for his contribution to *The Mirror for Magistrates* (p. 27).

[10] H. A. Watt, *Gorboduc; or, Ferrex and Porrex* (Madison, 1910), p. 53; it was R. A. Peters ("'Gorboduc' and Grafton's Chronicle," *Notes and Queries*, N. S. IV [1957], 333) who pointed out that *Gorboduc* precedes Grafton's version.

direct source of *Gorboduc*." [11] However, as Sister Maureen Walsh points out, there is much likelihood that the authors "may have relied on their memories of several versions and simply adapted the details to suit their needs." [12]

If the matter of the play is based on English chronicle history, the manner is based on two traditions, the Senecan and a native English dramatic tradition. Critics have long remarked on the tragedy's Senecan dependence: Schmidt declared that the "classical influence is due only to Seneca"; Cunliffe, although he later modified his view, attributed the form of the play, the long speeches, and the sententious precepts to Seneca; Schelling found the tragedy "pure Seneca"; and Watt asserted that "all the classical traces in *Gorboduc may* be due to the influence of the Senecan tragedies." [13] Howard Baker, dissenting from this "blighting critical fiction" of Seneca's influence, found the play closer to the moral play *Respublica* (1553) than to any Senecan play. [14] The best resolution between the full assertion of Seneca's influence and the denial of any is sounded by Marvin T. Herrick; he concludes that the predominant influence is Senecan, but that there are other classical influences—Virgil, Ovid, probably Statius, and possibly Plutarch and Lucan. [15]

The division of the play into five acts, the use of a chorus, a messenger, and other Senecan techniques show its kinship with the tradition; but as we shall see, it shows no blind acceptance of all the Senecan heritage. The usual Senecan themes—the danger of pride, the impetuosity of youth, the fickleness of fortune, the inexorability of fate, the certainty of death—are here in varying degrees and give rise—often too easily—to didacticism and heavy moralizing. As in Seneca, murder is followed by murder and revenge, and families fall (or claim they do) under an ancestral curse that dooms them to destruction. Because action is banished from the stage, the language

[11] *Thomas Sackville* (Groningen, 1948), p. 70.

[12] "Critical Edition," p. 75.

[13] H. Schmidt, "Seneca's Influence upon *Gorboduc*," *Modern Language Notes*, II (1887), 62; J. W. Cunliffe, *The Influence of Seneca on Elizabethan Tragedy* (London, 1893), p. 50; F. E. Schelling, *Elizabethan Drama* (Boston, 1908), II, 401; Watt, *Gorboduc*, p. 73.

[14] *Induction to Tragedy*, pp. 9–47.

[15] "Senecan Influence in *Gorboduc*," in *Studies in Speech and Drama in Honor of A. M. Drummond* (Ithaca, 1944), pp. 78–104. Other appraisals of Seneca's influence are in F. L. Lucas, *Seneca and Elizabethan Tragedy* (London, 1933); Theodore Spencer, *Death and Elizabethan Tragedy* (Harvard, 1936); and H. B. Charlton, *The Senecan Tradition* (Manchester, 1946).

becomes so highly rhetorical that it seems to us artificial and bombastic; it must substitute for the action itself, and we cannot quite share the intellectual excitement that may have come to an intelligent Elizabethan in listening to the language of the play. For us the monologues are much too long, and the stichomythia that would relieve them is ignored. The choruses that in Seneca would be lyrical and descriptive are here highly didactic, explicitly moralizing on the events of the preceding act. The chorus of four old men does not participate, as the chorus does in Seneca, in the action. The role of Nuntius, the messenger, is here played down, and Marcella, a minor character, performs his function in announcing Porrex's death. Revenge, one of the basic Senecan themes, is not introduced until Videna slays Porrex in the fourth act. The unities, an integral part of the Senecan technique, are here almost ignored except for the unity of fable. Where Senecan speeches aim at disclosing personal feelings, the speeches here are political and argumentative. Schelling was overstating the use of the tradition to call the play "pure Seneca." And we particularly miss the Senecan ghost, that characteristic part of his machinery that will become so useful to the later Elizabethans.

But *Gorboduc* shares in a native English dramatic tradition as well as a classical one. Willard Farnham[16] has pointed out that the play reminds us strongly of the moralities that had long been presented in England. The central character, a personification of a man of the world, is surrounded by allegorical characters, forces of good and of evil, who put forth arguments in favor of a virtuous or of a vicious life. Here we have a balancing of good and evil characters around Gorboduc and each of his sons; the balancing may be Senecan, as Farnham points out, but it is Senecan with a difference: it reproduces much of the effect obtained in the moralities when the forces of good and the forces of evil struggle for mastery over a human soul. He also notes that the play is as much the tragedy of a commonwealth as of a king, and thus it enforces a moral about the decay of the kingdom; in this way it is connected with a play like *Respublica* (1553), where the central character is Respublica herself, surrounded by Mercy, Justice, and Peace.[17]

[16] Farnham, *The Medieval Heritage of Elizabethan Tragedy* (Oxford, 1956), p. 353; see also Watt, *Gorboduc*, pp. 74–75, and Walsh, "Critical Edition," pp. 90–92.

[17] Professor Farnham notes that the fifth act would be a gross violation of dramatic unity unless it is intended to indicate that the authors conceive of the kingdom's having a dramatic entity (*Medieval Heritage*, p. 353).

The tragedy, in its morality aspect, may look further back to John Bale's *King John* (1538), rewritten as late as 1562 for royal presentation; there morality and history exist side by side. As Irving Ribner has pointed out,[18] *King John* is actually two plays at the same time. On one hand we have a political morality in the manner of Skelton's *Magnificence* or the anonymous *Albion Knight*, where Widow England is the central figure; on the other hand, we have a chronicle play adapted from English history. In *Gorboduc*, a play more tightly fused than *King John*, the king is a morality-like figure who stands for the unity of the commonwealth; when he is killed, the commonwealth passes into anarchy. But at the same time he is King Gorboduc, a human being who is husband and father as well as king. He is both allegorical and human.

The names of the counselors who surround him suggest their moral attributes: Eubulus, a traditional name for "wise counselor," Arostus, "flabby and weak," and Philander, "friend of mankind." "The counsellors are real figures," Professor Ribner writes, "but they are morality abstractions as well."[19] The play is a remarkable combination of a chronicle history and the morality tradition.

But beyond its kinship with the morality plays, *Gorboduc* shares in another English literary tradition, that made explicit in *The Mirror for Magistrates* (1559). That tradition is an expression of Tudor political philosophy and of history; it is a literary working-out of Amyot's description of history as "a certain rule and instruction, which by examples past, teacheth us to judge of things present and to foresee things to come: so we may know what to like of, and what to follow; what to mislike and what to eschew."[20] There is no doubt that the authors had this tradition in mind:

> And this great king, that doth divide his land
> > And change the course of his descending crown . . .
> A mirror shall become to princes all
> > To learn to shun the cause of such a fall.
>
> > > > > (I.ii.388–393)

All magistrates, the tradition declares, all those in authority, should

---

[18] Ribner, *The English History Play in the Age of Shakespeare* (London, 1965), pp. 45–46.

[19] Ibid., p. 47

[20] Quoted in L. B. Campbell, *Shakespeare's Histories* . . . (San Marino, 1947), p. 47.

look into the mirrors held up through poetry and drama to see how vice is punished, how retributive justice is inexorable. He who viewed the punishment of others would theoretically be brought to the self-examination of his own moral condition and, it was to be assumed, to the improvement of it. This was made explicit by the editor of *The Mirror*, William Baldwin, in the 1563 edition: "Here as in a looking glass, you shall see (if any vice be in you) how the like hath been punished in other heretofore; whereby admonished, I trust it will be a good occasion to move you to the sooner amendment."

The tragedy of King Gorboduc, a mirror that shows to a beholder what happens to a leaderless land, is the first dramatic embodiment of *The Mirror for Magistrates* tradition. By its use of this tradition, it joins—and rises above—the synthetic *de casibus* story, where the fall of man results from an arbitrary and capricious fate. Here fate collaborates with a man who makes an unwise decision, who abnegates his responsibilities, and who violates the laws of "kind," that primal nature that is the basis for one's living in a beneficent relationship with his fellow-man and with his God. By acting wisely and morally, this literary mirror points out, the tragedy that Gorboduc brings upon himself, his family, and his country could have been averted.

This kind of tradition, as exemplified in the drama, is a demonstration of the cause and effect that lies behind all of life. The dramatic effect, therefore, is reduced to reinforce the moral element. The authors do not invite us to become empathetic with the characters or with the events; we are not so much to live in the world of the play as to watch it. The characters are not to be thought of as much more than vehicles for the speeches; and if there are some briefly memorable characterizations, they are probably not deliberate. The persons do not matter as much as the descriptions of the political situation in which they find themselves. Norton and Sackville are not asking their viewers to involve themselves in an old British myth but to recognize the political import of the play. A stage filled with action would have distracted the Elizabethan viewers from the political thrust of the play. Those viewers—or those of us who are readers—must rather expect to observe the responses to all sorts of action, not action itself.

But if we are to be denied this involvement in the drama, we are invited to share another kind, the deliberate artistry, whose highest Elizabethan name is artifice, of two young men in their attempt to appeal to a sophisticated audience. And there are several kinds of artistry that should not be missed. The first reading of the play, less than 1800 lines long, may produce the kind of response that prompted F. L. Lucas to say that it belongs to antiquarianism rather than to literature.[21] Such a response dismisses too lightly the conscious craftsmanship of the play. Moreover, another response (perhaps a rather common one), that the play moves exceedingly slowly, can be as misleading. Actually, when the plot is summarized, the drama appears to move with urgent precipitousness: in the first scene, the king, who is sincerely interested in his country's welfare, discloses his plan, and despite advice to the contrary, he carries it out in the second scene. The second act describes the coming of the civil war; Ferrex is killed by the end of the third act. The fourth act, temporarily slowed down by the aria-lament of Videna, is followed by Porrex's trial and his murder. In the fifth act, the king and the queen are already dead, the country is plunged into chaos, and the state is destroyed. But despite all this action, it is the response to the action that is set forth, not the action itself. What has been deliberately chosen is the "point of rest" between actual incidents that are carefully omitted. "The essential thing is not what happens," Wolfgang Clemen writes, "but the political and moral implications of what happens."[22]

Another kind of artifice is the synthetic balance in the parts of the play. After the foreboding of the opening scene between Videna and Ferrex, the division of the kingdom takes place. Gorboduc makes his unwise decision after advice from three counselors, each of whom expresses a clear point of view in an appropriate space: Arostus is quick to approve, Philander argues delay, and Eubulus dissents from the plan. Nearly equal time has been shared by each adviser.[23] In the second act, first at the court of Ferrex and then at the court of Porrex, two advisers, one foolish and the other wise, argue for and against going to war. In the third act, Gorboduc hears of his sons' actions, first through the letter of Dordan concerning Ferrex, and second, through Philander, who reports directly concerning Porrex. In the fourth act, Videna's lament for the murdered Ferrex is balanced against Marcella's account of the murder of Porrex. And in the last

[21] *Seneca and Elizabethan Tragedy*, p. 96.

[22] Clemen, *English Tragedy Before Shakespeare* (London, 1961), p. 62.

[23] See Clemen, p. 64, for an analysis of the rhetoric of these speeches.

act, Arostus and Eubulus vie in bemoaning the fallen realm and its royalty. The play is carefully balanced between differing points of view and varying responses to action.[24]

Another kind of artifice may be seen in the dumb shows, descended either from the Italian dramatic tradition, the *intermedii*, or adapted from court masques or the city pageants. Highly allegorical in nature, they foreshadow the events of the ensuing acts. In the first dumb show, the sticks that are joined cannot be broken; but divided, they easily can be: the kingdom united is secure; but divided, it is easily destroyed. In the second dumb show, the king who chooses the gold cup rather than the glass falls prey to flattery, even as Ferrex and Porrex do. In the third dumb show, the mourners are preparing us for the death of Ferrex; and in the fourth dumb show, the procession of mourners and murderers of their children is but prelude to the three murders that follow. And in the last dumb show, the armed men and those who discharge their harquebusses signify the rebellions that are to follow. In each instance the musical instruments accompanying the dumb show are appropriate. The violins (I) set the mood of the play; the cornets (II) are a proper flourish after the division of the kingdom and before the establishment of the princes in their own state; the sound of flutes (III) is appropriate for mourning; oboes (IV) are still described as having a mournful sound; and drums and flutes (V) are traditionally martial. Whether an expositor patiently explained the dumb shows or whether the sophisticated audience could interpret them unaided, the play gives no hint. But, like the play itself, the aim of the dumb shows is evident—to bring out a moral.

Still another kind of artifice is the emphatic insistence upon *kind*, or *kindliness*, sometimes paraphrased as *nature*.[25] The words express the Elizabethan concept of sound principles or common-sense actions. When a person acts *unkindly*, he is going against sound principles, is violating a natural common sense. Gorboduc, who is described as "unkind" but never as evil, commits an error by acting "unkindly," by going against good advice, by unnaturally dividing his elder son's heritage, by undertaking a precipitate action to renounce his

[24] It is interesting to note the balance in the lines themselves; for example, see II.i.143 and III.i.171 for balanced alliteration; III.i.54–55 for balanced clauses; IV.ii.117 for balanced modifiers; and IV.ii.166 for balanced rhetorical questions.

[25] *Kind* and its variants (*kindliness, unkind, unkindly*) appear thirty-seven times in the play; *nature* and its variant *unnatural* appear twenty times.

responsibilities as king. His sons, in turn, are given to "randon," to acting without restraint, without due regard for the proprieties of rule and realm. And if king and princes act so unkindly, the commonwealth will respond with unnatural acts. For king *is* commonwealth, and royal family corresponds to the state. When the realm is guided by the unkindly, the unnatural, it is sure to suffer.

A final artifice concerns the myth and legend exploited by the authors. Early in the play (I.ii.162) the reference to Morgan, who warred with his cousin Cunedag for the kingdom, foreshadows the inevitable civil war between the brothers, should Gorboduc divide his kingdom. Only three lines later, the reference to Brutus reminds us that we are watching a drama of the descendants of the legendary founder of Britain, an epilogue to the story of Troy. Brutus had divided his kingdom among his sons, but they inherited only after his death. Nevertheless, wars ensued; the kingdom was plagued by a divided realm. Now that story is being repeated; the glib Arostus, the ingratiating Philander both quickly approve Gorboduc's plan; the good counselor Eubulus sees the unnaturalness of the act. The story of Brutus is being played out again; the implicit hope for the realm of 1562 is that the story will not be played out another time.

In the same scene (I.ii.330–332), again in the scene's concluding chorus (I.ii.385–387), and in II.i.204, the story of Phaeton is an exemplum told to remind us of the indulgence of Gorboduc and the rashness of the brothers in assuming rule of the kingdom. Phaeton, who seized his father Apollo's horses too soon, brought ruin to himself and to the earth; thus the premature rule of Ferrex and Porrex brings ruin to them and to the land. They both hear good and foolish advice in turn; like Phaeton, they undertake a rash act, heedless of good advice. They are young, inexperienced, foolish, and unwise.

Early in the second act (II.i.16–17) the invocation of Tantalus and Ixion as curses ironically reflects the attitudes both of Ferrex, who speaks these lines, and of Porrex. Tantalus, the human being who wishes to rise above his basic humanity, sacrifices his family to his own ambition. Ferrex arouses enough suspicion in the ambitious Porrex so that he is murdered; tantalizingly, the fruits of the crown do not descend to Porrex. The selfishness and stupidity of Ixion bring forth a frustrating result, a race of centaurs as well as punishment in Hell. His story has its evident kinship with the brothers' actions.

Gorboduc's comparison of himself and his queen to Priam and Hecuba (III.i.14–16) elevates his tragedy to theirs and links again

– xxii –

his story with the fall of Troy. And finally, the procession of child-murderers, whipped on by the Furies (Dumb Show IV) anticipates the unnatural murders to follow. These, the most unnatural of criminals, are equated with the criminals of Gorboduc's family and suggest the responsibility that Gorboduc himself plays in the deaths of his wife and their two sons: the' dumb show indicates the punishment in store for them all.

All these mythological references have to do with the rule of self and of the realm. Gorboduc, like Brutus and Morgan, errs in ruling and plunges the realm, through his unnatural decision, into civil war. Ferrex and Porrex, like Phaeton, assume rule before they are ready for it; destruction follows. Again, they, like Tantalus and Ixion, are so filled with ambition that they condemn themselves to an infinity of punishment. Finally, Gorboduc and his queen join the six child-murderers, driven by the Furies, because they have acted, like the murderers, through anger, jealousy, and rashness. The impact of the mythology, like the political basis of the play, is essentially moral. Gorboduc, like his mythological referents, releases forces upon his life, his family, and his kingdom that can only destroy. The release of these forces spawns a Fergus, Duke of Albany, whose ambitions will serve as scourge to the kingdom.

THE POLITICAL INTENT

Two matters have occupied most political analyses of the drama: first, that it was highly admonitory about how Elizabeth should act; and second, that a discussion of the play must include a detailed tracing of the great question of succession to the crown. The first matter may quickly be dealt with: Elizabeth was not at the play's first performance, and perhaps it would have been given no second performance if the royal curiosity had not been piqued. To have admonished her in specific terms about how she should act would have been both impolitic and impertinent. Even at her young age, for she was less than thirty in 1562, she did not easily suffer gratuitous advice. What the play is saying is argumentative—that Parliament should see to it that succession to the crown is made clear—rather than admonitory. If there is a subject for any admonition the play contains, it is Parliament and the Queen's council. We know that the council was at the Twelfth Night performance; Machyn tells us of their presence. The Queen was not there, and presumably she was not expected. It is hard to admonish someone who is absent.

Second, the play is written against the background of Elizabeth's first Parliament, that of 1559. That Parliament dealt successfully with the matter of religion, but it did briefly consider the matter of succession. To discuss the play in the light of Elizabeth's second Parliament (1563), which dealt much more fully with the succession, or by reference to later Parliaments, is to read into it more than we should. Thus the matter of succession need not be traced through all the Parliamentary entanglements when we are examining a play of 1561–1562.

However, we need to see how Elizabeth came to the throne and how her father had provided for the succession to the crown.[26] Henry's decree, confirmed by Parliament by the Act of 1543, established the order of succession as Edward and his issue, Mary and her issue, and Elizabeth and her issue; it further provided that Henry could appoint further successors in his last will. In that will he named the descendants of his younger sister, his nieces Lady Frances Brandon and her heirs and Lady Eleanor Brandon and her heirs, as his successors on the default of any lawful issue of his three children. By naming these descendants, those in the Suffolk line, he voided the hereditary claims of the Stuarts, the descendants of his elder sister.

When Edward died, the Duke of Northumberland unsuccessfully tried to place Lady Jane Grey, oldest daughter of Lady Frances Brandon, on the throne by virtue of her nomination by Edward. But Henry's will held firm, and Mary ascended the throne by virtue of the Act of 1543 and "the last will of our dearest father." Obviously that Act and the will were looked upon as impressive constitutional arguments against Northumberland's attempt.

When Elizabeth came to the throne, her presumptive successor was Lady Catherine Grey, Lady Jane's sister. However, in 1560

[26] In discussing the political aspect of the play, I am much indebted, as will be obvious, to Sir John Neale, *Elizabeth I and Her Parliaments 1559–1581* (London, 1953); Mortimer Levine, *The Early Elizabethan Succession Question 1558–1568* (Stanford, 1966) and his "A Parliamentary Title to the Crown in Tudor England," *Huntington Library Quarterly*, XXV (1962), 121–127; and Ernest W. Talbert, "The Political Import and the First Two Audiences of *Gorboduc*," in *Studies in Honor of DeWitt T. Starnes* (Austin, 1967), pp. 89–115.

Lady Catherine had clandestinely married Edward Seymour, the Earl of Hertford, son of the Protestant Protector Somerset of Edward's reign. Elizabeth—and others—could rightly have feared an alliance between the powerful Seymours, and the Greys, particularly after the birth of their son in September, 1561. Although Lady Catherine had her adherents in the council, other members supported the Earl of Huntington, a staunch Protestant; but to name him to the succession, despite his descent from a younger brother of Edward IV, would have violated Henry's will. Others were also named—Lady Margaret Strange, Lady Margaret Lennox, and, of course, Mary Stuart. Lady Catherine was seen by the Protestants as a safeguard of their faith; Mary Stuart was seen by the Roman Catholics as the assured restorer of theirs.

Into the arguments over the succession was introduced an allegation that Henry's will had not been properly executed, that it had been signed with a stamp rather than by the king's "most gracious hand"; but there was no doubt that the crown could be disposed of only by Parliament's own action. William Atwood declared that "it is . . . certain that King Henry should have had no authority or power to dispose of the crown by will if by Parliament it had not been given him." But Parliament had conferred the crown both on Mary and Elizabeth, both of whom had been bastardized by the Act of 1536. What is important is that Parliament, recognizing their bastardy—i.e., that they could not inherit property, being the child of no one—still conferred the crown upon them. They did not inherit the crown through hereditary rights but through an act of Parliament. But before the Parliament was to move to consider any way of appointing a successor to Elizabeth, it was to urge her to marry.

On February 4, 1559, the Commons heard arguments that Elizabeth be requested to marry, and two days later a group of members, the Speaker, and the privy-councilors were admitted to her presence. We are told that the Speaker "solemnly and eloquently set forth the message." It is likely that the members suggested that she marry within the realm by choosing an Englishman; but as Elizabeth pointed out in her reply, the message contained no limitation of place or person. The Queen responded to her petitioners while they were in audience, but she probably asked them to withhold a report of their meeting with her until the authentic text of her reply could reach them. Four days later it did. It is a message that is evasive, distinctive, regally politic, but it let them know that she was not blind to the question of the succession.[27] However, she gave them no real hope either of marrying or of appointing a successor. As we now know, she did not marry and did not appoint her successor until she lay on her deathbed.[28]

There were other matters, not just that of the succession, that indicated a Parliament ever loyal but determined upon having a part in the ruling of England. No one could think that Parliament could act without the Queen, but the Commons must have thought that Henry's actions set a precedent for their part in naming Elizabeth's successor. Certainly they could discuss possible candidates, even accepting or rejecting nominations presented to them. For Elizabeth, on the other hand, an immediate succession settlement was out of the question.[29] She probably desired to see no succession settlement at all; she objected to one claimant, Lady Catherine Grey, favored by the Commons; if the settlement excluded the Stuarts, England could face a difficult international situation; no one who could be named would be universally accepted in England; and finally, she probably thought that the problem was one for the crown to solve, not the Commons. Their determination to settle the matter was equaled only by the Queen's determination not to settle it.

But in 1562, she had received only one petition from Parliament, and she was probably at that time not opposed to the lines in *Gorboduc* that speak of the part that Parliament should play in determining her successor.[30] Arostus urges (V.ii.157–179) the calling of Parliament and the settling of the matter. The kingdom, of course, at that point in the play is leaderless, and thus there can be no talk of the coöperation of crown and Commons. But the passage seems to insist on several matters that, by analogy, the first audience must have noticed: first, Arostus declares that Parliament should respect the right of the candidates for the crown, and he makes explicit what "right" it is he is urging—the right of "native line" and the "virtue of some former

[27] The reply, transcribed from Neale, *Elizabeth I*, pp. 48–50, is given in Appendix A.

[28] Parliaments were to continue in 1563 and 1566 to question Elizabeth about the succession until she finally ordered them to speak of it no more; such an abridgement of the freedom of their speech angered the Parliament of 1566 so much that Elizabeth, needing money, had to abandon her objections. The petition of 1563 was read to her by Thomas Norton, and there are verbal similarities between it and the play he helped to write.

[29] Levine, *Succession Question*, p. 195.

[30] Talbert, "Political Import," p. 106.

law." Most likely such words could be interpreted as support for Lady Catherine Grey, a native nominated by the will of Henry. Certainly, as the speech concludes, Arostus is distinctly opposed to any "foreign prince," perhaps not so much a reference to Mary Stuart as a reflection of a general theory of statecraft, expressed by Erasmus and others, that would favor a prince born and bred among those he is to rule.

But Arostus's words are not the last. Eubulus, the wise counselor, sums up the political moral:

> . . . parliament should have been holden,
> And certain heirs appointed to the crown,
> To stay the title of established right
> And in the people plant obedience
> While yet the prince did live whose name and power
> By lawful summons and authority
> Might make a parliament to be of force
> And might have set the state in quiet stay.
>
> (V.ii.264–271)

These lines belie the assumption that *Gorboduc* was an admonition to the Queen alone; they point out the necessity for a working together by both crown and Parliament to choose a successor. And obviously it should thus be done during the ruler's life so that the people will be planted in obedience to the successor.

The play, then, is a plea for this mutual and wise solution about the succession. Unless a solution is reached, the play is saying, England might face the same kind of civil strife that followed Brutus's reign, Gorboduc's reign, and, by extension, other reigns—such as Elizabeth's—where the succession was not decided; but emphatically the decision must be one of wisdom. Brutus and Gorboduc both provided for the succession, but the provision was unwise. Such wisdom will allow England to avoid the horrors of rebellion and civil war. In a homily such as *Against Disobedience and Willful Rebellion* (1570), the general attitude of the Elizabethans toward rebellion is seen:

How horrible a thing against God and man rebellion is, cannot possibly be expressed according to the greatness thereof. He that nameth rebellion nameth not a singular or one only sin, as in theft, robbery, murder, and such like; but he nameth the whole puddle and sink of all sins against God and man; against his prince, his country, his countrymen, his parents, his children, his kinfolks, against God and all men heaped together nameth he that nameth rebellion.[31]

A monarch who rashly brings his subjects into rebelling against him "nameth the whole puddle and sink of all sins" by his action.

But beyond these arguments about the settlement of the succession, the play has something to say about the nature of the ruler.[32] The play expresses concepts that are almost commonplace about the possessor of kingly power. He is appointed by God, receives authority from Him, and thus is responsible to God. He exists for the welfare and wealth of those he governs and for no other purpose. If he misuses his power, God will punish him. In the punishment of the ruler, his nation will also suffer; he is not only a man, but the head of the commonwealth, indivisible from it.

The ruler, moreover, must so reign that he will pass his honor on to his sons, particularly in keeping of the "common peace" (I.ii.22). In order to reign honorably, he must obey good advice. When he disobeys such advice, he insures punishment not only for himself, but also for his family and his nation. Thus, when Gorboduc bows his head to his sons, despite Philander's advice, and divides his kingdom, despite Eubulus's advice, he is determining his own fate and that of the kingdom.

The tragedy may seem to be a somber way of celebrating the festivities of the Christmas season, but there is no doubt that it spoke of matters close to Elizabeth's subjects. In 1561–1562 they must have been highly concerned over what could befall them if she died or made an improper marriage or appointed an undeserving successor. From hindsight we know that Elizabeth's reign did not end in a catastrophe but in triumph. But in 1562 the authors of *Gorboduc*, remembering the cruelties of Mary and her foreign marriage, could not be so confident of Elizabeth's wisdom and of her success as we can be.

[31] Quoted in Ribner, *English History Play*, p. 309.

[32] Professor Talbert ("Political Import," pp. 93 ff.) has effectively countered the arguments of Sara Ruth Watson, "*Gorboduc* and the Theory of Tyrannicide," *Modern Language Review*, XXXIV (1939), 355–366. He has shown that Norton and Sackville probably agreed on certain basic concepts, some of them here mentioned, and the division of their thought that Miss Watson finds in the play now appears to have been overstated.

THE TEXT

The first publication of the play (Q1) is dated September 22, 1565, from the shop of William Griffith in St. Dunstan's Churchyard "in the West of London." The title page gives us the details of its authorship and of its presentation before the Queen:

> THE/ TRAGEDIE OF GORBODVC;/ whereof three Actes were wrytten by/ *Thomas Nortone*, and the two laste by/ *Thomas Sackuyle.*/ Sett forthe as the same was shewed before the/ *QVENES* most excellent Maiestie, in her highnes/ Court of Whitehall, the xviii. day of January,/ *Anno Domini.* 1561. By the Gentlemen/ of Thynner Temple in London.

The title page of the second edition (Q2, 1570), that coming from John Day's shop "over Aldersgate," confirms the date of presentation but is silent on the attribution of authorship:

> The Tragidie of Ferrex/ and Porrex,/ set forth without addition or alte-/ ration but altogether as the same was shewed/ on stage before the Queenes Maiestie,/ about nine yeares past, *vz.* the/ xviij. day of Ianuarie. 1561./ by the gentlemen of the/ Inner Temple.

Traditionally, the titles given on the two title pages have been combined to give the play its title—*Gorboduc, or Ferrex and Porrex.*

In the address to the reader in Q2, John Day, its printer, arraigns William Griffith, the printer of Q1, for his piracy and his corruption of the text. The first quarto had been printed from copy supplied by an unauthorized source, it appears; the second quarto had followed because of the authors' dissatisfaction with the errors of the first. But, despite that dissatisfaction and Day's hyperbolical address, Q1 was not so corrupt that, if corrected, it could not be used for the copy-text for Q2.[33]

There are some one hundred and eighty substantive changes made in Q1 readings for Q2. But Q2 retains at least five of Q1's errors and introduces some nine manifest errors of its own. Moreover, Q2 omits an eight-line passage, perhaps for political reasons.

---

[33] Sir Walter Greg in his *Bibliography of the English Printed Drama to the Restoration* (I, 115) declared that "there can be little doubt that [Q2] was set up from a corrected copy of [Q1]." My "*Gorboduc, Ferrex and Porrex:* The First Two Quartos," *Studies in Bibliography*, XV (1962), 231–233, resolves, I trust, even that "little doubt."

But there is no doubt that, for an edition in modern spelling, Q2 is the evident choice for the copy-text. The scribe that prepared the copy-text for John Day, even though he was correcting the corrupt Q1, moved slowly and carefully in his duties. He restored omitted words and corrected evident misreadings; he regularized the meter and substituted words and phrases that, in context, seem to be superior to the Q1 readings. But the strongest persuader for using Q2 as our copy-text is John Day himself who, in his message to the reader, assures us that he has tried to put new apparel on a "dis-honested" body. There is no reason to think that he has not succeeded.

For this edition I have collated copies of Q2 from these collections: Bodleian (Malone 257), Harvard (two copies), Pforzheimer, Yale, and the New York Public Library. Microfilms of these copies have been carefully compared with the British Museum copy in Farmer's Tudor Facsimile Text (London, 1908), my control copy. The collation brought to light three variant readings, evidently caused by press correction, on B2, B2^v, and E3^v, none of them important. For Q3, which save for some egregious sophistication is a reprint of Q1, I have used the Folger Library copy. I am most grateful to these libraries and to the staff of the Alderman Library, University of Virginia, for their generous assistance. To express my gratitude to Professor Fredson Bowers and to the general editor of this series, Professor Hoy, for their encouragement and their help can hardly indicate the measure of my indebtedness to them.

The punctuation of Q2 is at times more than confusing; the present text is punctuated as lightly as I believe possible. In view of the large number of rhetorically florid sentences, I hope the light punc-tuation will clarify the meaning and not intrude upon the reader. All of the speakers within a scene are given in the quartos at the beginning of each scene; I have rather followed modern practice. I have not tried to remedy the quartos' paucity of stage directions; the scarcity of them will surely strike a modern reader.

I hope that this present edition will make evident the features of *Gorboduc*'s style—"a propriety in the sentiments, dignity in the sentences, and an unaffected perspicuity of style . . . in a word, that chastity, correctness, and gravity of style which are so essential to tragedy." According to Robert Dodsley, this was the praise of the drama from Alexander Pope.

IRBY B. CAUTHEN, JR.

University of Virginia

GORBODUC
OR
FERREX AND PORREX

The Argument of the Tragedy

Gorboduc, King of Britain, divided his realm in his lifetime to his sons, Ferrex and Porrex. The sons fell to dissension. The younger killed the elder. The mother, that more dearly loved the elder, for revenge killed the younger. The people, moved with the cruelty of the fact, rose in 5 rebellion and slew both father and mother. The nobility assembled and most terribly destroyed the rebels. And afterwards, for want of issue of the Prince, whereby the succession of the crown became uncertain, they fell to civil war, in which both they and many of their issues were slain, and the 10 land for a long time almost desolate and miserably wasted.

3. dissension] *Q 2;* dyuision and   tion *Q 3.*
discention *Q 1;* deuision and dissen-

---

5. *fact*] "an evil deed, a crime" (*OED*).
8–11. for . . . wasted] an indication of the cautionary political aspect of the play.

The P[rinter] to the Reader

Where this tragedy was for furniture of part of the grand
Christmas in the Inner Temple, first written about nine years
ago by the right honorable Thomas, now Lord Buckhurst,
and by T. Norton, and after showed before her Majesty, and
never intended by the authors thereof to be published; yet   5
one W. G., getting a copy thereof at some young man's hand
that lacked a little money and much discretion, in the last
great plague, an[no] 1565, about five years past, while the said
Lord was out of England, and T. Norton far out of London,
and neither of them both made privy, put it forth exceed-   10
ingly corrupted—even as if by means of a broker, for hire, he
should have enticed into his house a fair maid and done her
villainy, and after all to-bescratched her face, torn her apparel, bewrayed and disfigured her, and then thrust her out
of doors dishonested. In such plight, after long wandering,   15
she came at length home to the sight of her friends, who scant
knew her but by a few tokens and marks remaining. They,
the authors I mean, though they were very much displeased
that she so ran abroad without leave, whereby she caught
her shame, as many wantons do, yet seeing the case, as it is,   20
remediless, have for common honesty and shamefastness new
appareled, trimmed, and attired her in such form as she was
before. In which better form since she hath come to me, I
have harbored her for her friends' sake and her own, and I
do not doubt her parents, the authors, will not now be dis-   25
content that she go abroad among you good readers, so it be
in honest company. For she is by my encouragement and
others' somewhat less ashamed of the dishonesty done to her
because it was by fraud and force. If she be welcome among
you and gently entertained, in favor of the house from   30

0.1–40. The . . . withal.] *Q 2; not in
Q 1, Q 3.*

---

1. *furniture*] provision, decoration.
6. *W. G.*] William Gifford, the printer of Q1.
11. *broker*] pander, go-between (Nares).
13. *to-bescratched*] very much scratched.
14. *bewrayed*] betrayed.
15. *dishonested*] dishonored.

whence she is descended and of her own nature courteously
disposed to offend no man, her friends will thank you for it.
If not, but that she shall be still reproached with her former
mishap or quarreled at by envious persons, she, poor gentle-
woman, will surely play Lucrece's part and of herself die for 35
shame, and I shall wish that she had tarried still at home
with me, where she was welcome; for she did never put me
to more charge, but this one poor black gown lined with
white that I have now given her to go abroad among you
withal. 40

35. *Lucrece*] "That singular pattern of chastity" who, ravished by Tarquin,
revealed the "shameful reproach and infamy" to her family and then killed
herself, "affirming that the example of Lucrece should never be a cloak for
light women to excuse the unfaithful breach of wedlock" (Starnes and
Talbot).
38–39. *black gown . . . white*] i.e., this book.

THE NAMES OF THE SPEAKERS

GORBODUC, *King of Great Britain*
VIDENA, *Queen and wife to King Gorboduc*
FERREX, *elder son to King Gorboduc*
PORREX, *younger son to King Gorboduc*
CLOTYN, *Duke of Cornwall*   5
FERGUS, *Duke of Albany*
MANDUD, *Duke of Logris*
GWENARD, *Duke of Camberland*
EUBULUS, *Secretary to the King*
AROSTUS, *a counselor to the King*   10
DORDAN, *a counselor assigned by the King to his eldest son, Ferrex*
PHILANDER, *a counselor assigned by the King to his youngest son,*
   Porrex; both being of the old King's council before
HERMON, *a parasite remaining with Ferrex*
TYNDAR, *a parasite remaining with Porrex*   15
NUNTIUS, *a messenger of the elder brother's death*
NUNTIUS, *a messenger of Duke Fergus' rising in arms*
MARCELLA, *a lady of the Queen's privy-chamber*
CHORUS, *four ancient and sage men of Britain*

[Scene, Britain]   20

5. CLOTYN] *Q 1, Q 3;* Cloyton *Q 2.*
7. *Logris*] Loegris *Q 2;* Leagre *Q 1,*
Q 3.
8. *Camberland*] *this edn.;* Cumber-
land *Q 2;* Cumperlande *Q 1;* Cum-
berlande *Q 3.*

9. *King*] *Q 2;* kynge *Gorboduc Q 1,*
Q 3.
10. *to the King*] *Q 2;* of kinge *Gor-*
boduc Q 1, Q 3.
12. *youngest*] *Q 2;* yonger *Q 1, Q 3.*

7. *Logris*] an old name for England. Geoffrey of Monmouth (II.i) records the portioning out of Britain to Brutus's three sons: Locrinus was given Logris (or Logria), Camber was given Cambria (now Wales), and Albanact was given Albania (now Scotland). As a descendant of Cunedag (see I.ii.162, note), Gorboduc governed the whole island.

8. *Camberland*] Q1–2 agree (at I.ii.163) that the spelling should be Camberland; "Camber had that part which lieth beyond the river Severn, and is now called Wales, which afterward was for a long time called Cambria, after his name" (Geoffrey of Monmouth, II.i). Swart confirms this reading.

9. *Secretary*] "one who is entrusted with private or secret matters" (*OED*).

14. *parasite*] "one who eats at the table or at the expense of another . . . one who obtains the hospitality, patronage, or favor of the wealthy by obsequiousness and flattery" (*OED*).

The Order of the Dumb Show Before the First Act, and the Signification Thereof

First, the music of violins began to play, during which came in upon the stage six wild men clothed in leaves. Of whom the first bare on his neck a fagot of small sticks, which they all, both severally and together, assayed with all their strengths to break; but it could not be broken by them. At   5 the length, one of them plucked out one of the sticks, and brake it; and the rest plucking out all the other sticks one after another, did easily break them, the same being severed; which being conjoined, they had before attempted in vain. After they had this done, they departed the stage, and the   10 music ceased. Hereby was signified that a state knit in unity doth continue strong against all force, but being divided, is easily destroyed; as befell upon King Gorboduc dividing his land to his two sons, which he before held in monarchy, and upon the dissension of the brethren, to whom it was divided.   15

3. on] *Q 3;* in *Q 1–2.*
6. plucked] *Q 1–2;* pulled *Q 3, Sackville-West.*

8. them] *Q 2; not in Q 1, Q 3.*
13. King] *this edn., conjecture, Scott;* Duke *Q 1–3.*

2. *wild men*] These "wodewoses" were common figures in folk plays, masques, and the like, costumed as satyrs, fauns, savages, and similar primitive, rustic characters. Here they seem to symbolize a primitive Britain (Walsh) or a kind of rudimentary common sense.

3. *fagot*] The ultimate source of this device is Aesop, but it is commonplace in proverbial lore (see Tilley, K 89 and U 11). Herrick sees in this dumb show a dramatic representation of a line of Lydgate's, "Kingdoms divided may no while endure."

Gorboduc
or
Ferrex and Porrex

[I.i]   [*Enter*] Videna [*and*] Ferrex.

VIDENA.

The silent night that brings the quiet pause
From painful travails of the weary day
Prolongs my careful thoughts and makes me blame
The slow Aurore, that so for love or shame
Doth long delay to show her blushing face;   5
And now the day renews my griefful plaint.

FERREX.

My gracious lady and my mother dear,
Pardon my grief for your so grieved mind
To ask what cause tormenteth so your heart.

VIDENA.

So great a wrong and so unjust despite   10
Without all cause against all course of kind!

FERREX.

Such causeless wrong and so unjust despite
May have redress or, at the least, revenge.

---

7. my] *Q 2; not in Q 1, Q 3.*

1–6. *The . . . plaint*] from Seneca, *Octavia*, ll. 1–6, *Oedipus*, ll. 1–5, *Hercules Furens*, ll. 125–140, and *Agamemnon*, ll. 53–56 (Cunliffe); Herrick compares Ovid *Amores* I. xiii. 36; Lydgate, *Troy Book*, III.5–9, and Virgil *Aeneid* iv. 527.

2. *travails*] toil.

3. *careful*] full of care or sorrow.

4. *Aurore*] Aurora, goddess of the dawn.

6. *griefful*] full of grief.

10. *despite*] insult.

11. *kind*] nature.

VIDENA.

> Neither, my son; such is the froward will,
> The person such, such my mishap and thine. 15

FERREX.

> Mine know I none, but grief for your distress.

VIDENA.

> Yes, mine for thine, my son. A father? No.
> In kind a father, not in kindliness.

FERREX.

> My father? Why? I know nothing at all
> Wherein I have misdone unto his grace. 20

VIDENA.

> Therefore the more unkind to thee and me.
> For, knowing well, my son, the tender love
> That I have ever borne and bear to thee,
> He, grieved thereat, is not content alone
> To spoil me of thy sight, my chiefest joy, 25
> But thee of thy birthright and heritage,
> Causeless, unkindly, and in wrongful wise,
> Against all law and right, he will bereave.
> Half of his kingdom he will give away.

FERREX.

> To whom?

VIDENA.   Even to Porrex, his younger son, 30

> Whose growing pride I do so sore suspect
> That, being raised to equal rule with thee,
> Methinks I see his envious heart to swell,
> Filled with disdain and with ambitious hope.
> The end the gods do know, whose altars I 35

---

18. not] *Q 2;* but not *Q 1, Q 3.*
25. me of thy] *Dodsley;* thee of my *Q 1–3.*

26. birthright] *Q 2;* birth, right *Q 1;* birth-right *Q 3.*
34. hope] *Q 2;* pride *Q 1, Q 3.*

14. *froward*] stubborn, refractory.
18. *kind . . . kindliness*] "This line exemplifies the Elizabethan meaning of *kind,* i.e. *nature,* as well as the secondary meaning for which it stands in modern use. Cf. Shakespeare's play on the word 'A little more than kin, and less than kind' (*Hamlet* I.ii.65)" (Smith).
25. *spoil*] deprive.
27. *unkindly*] unnaturally.
28. *bereave*] take away by force.

Full oft have made in vain of cattle slain
To send the sacred smoke to Heaven's throne
For thee, my son, if things do so succeed,
As now my jealous mind misdeemeth sore.

FERREX.

Madam, leave care and careful plaint for me.   40
Just hath my father been to every wight.
His first unjustice he will not extend
To me, I trust, that give no cause thereof.
My brother's pride shall hurt himself, not me.

VIDENA.

So grant the gods! But yet thy father so   45
Hath firmly fixed his unmoved mind
That plaints and prayers can no whit avail;
For those have I assayed, but even this day
He will endeavor to procure assent
Of all his council to his fond devise.   50

FERREX.

Their ancestors from race to race have borne
True faith to my forefathers and their seed;
I trust they eke will bear the like to me.

VIDENA.

There resteth all. But if they fail thereof,
And if the end bring forth an ill success,   55
On them and theirs the mischief shall befall.
And so I pray the gods requite it them;
And so they will, for so is wont to be
When lords and trusted rulers under kings,
To please the present fancy of the prince,   60
With wrong transpose the course of governance,
Murders, mischief, or civil sword at length,

---

38. do] *Q 2; not in Q 1, Q 3.*   55. ill] *Q 2;* euyll *Q 1, Q 3.*

---

39. *jealous*] suspicious.
39. *misdeemeth sore*] greatly fears.
48. *assayed*] tried.
50. *fond devise*] foolish plan.
53. *eke*] also.
55. *success*] outcome.
57. *requite*] "to repay, make retaliation or return for, to avenge (a wrong, injury, etc.)" (*OED*).

Or mutual treason or a just revenge,
When right succeeding line returns again,
By Jove's just judgment and deserved wrath,   65
Brings them to cruel and reproachful death
And roots their names and kindreds from the earth.

FERREX.

Mother, content you, you shall see the end.

VIDENA.

The end? Thy end, I fear; Jove end me first.   [*Exeunt.*]

[I.ii]   [*Enter*] Gorboduc, Arostus, Philander, [*and*] Eubulus.

GORBODUC.

My lords, whose grave advice and faithful aid
Have long upheld my honor and my realm
And brought me to this age from tender years,
Guiding so great estate with great renown,
Now more importeth me than erst to use   5
Your faith and wisdom, whereby yet I reign;
That, when by death my life and rule shall cease,
The kingdom yet may with unbroken course
Have certain prince by whose undoubted right
Your wealth and peace may stand in quiet stay;   10
And eke that they whom nature hath prepared
In time to take my place in princely seat,
While in their father's time their pliant youth
Yields to the frame of skilful governance,
May so be taught and trained in noble arts,   15
As what their fathers, which have reigned before,
Have with great fame derived down to them,
With honor they may leave unto their seed;

66. cruel] *Q2;* ciuill *Q1, Q3;* evill   3. from] *Q1–2;* and *Q3:*
Dodsley.   5. than] *Q2;* the *Q1, Q3;* then
[I.ii]   *Dodsley.*
3. to] *Q2;* from *Q1, Q3.*   10. in] *Q1–2;* at *Q3.*

5. *Now . . . me*] It is more important to me.
5. *erst*] formerly.
10. *stay*] "a permanent state or condition" (*OED*).
17. *derived*] descended.

And not be thought, for their unworthy life
And for their lawless swerving out of kind,   20
Worthy to lose what law and kind them gave;
But that they may preserve the common peace,
The cause that first began and still maintains
The lineal course of kings' inheritance,
For me, for mine, for you, and for the state   25
Whereof both I and you have charge and care.
Thus do I mean to use your wonted faith
To me and mine and to your native land.
My lords, be plain without all wry respect
Or poisonous craft to speak in pleasing wise,   30
Lest as the blame of ill-succeeding things
Shall light on you, so light the harms also.

AROSTUS.

Your good acceptance so, most noble king,
Of such our faithfulness as heretofore
We have employed in duties to your grace   35
And to this realm, whose worthy head you are,
Well proves that neither you mistrust at all,
Nor we shall need in boasting wise to show
Our truth to you nor yet our wakeful care
For you, for yours, and for our native land.   40
Wherefore, O king, I speak as one for all,
Sith all as one do bear you egal faith:
Doubt not to use our counsels and our aids,
Whose honors, goods, and lives are whole avowed
To serve, to aid, and to defend your grace.   45

GORBODUC.

My lords, I thank you all. This is the case:
Ye know, the gods, who have the sovereign care
For kings, for kingdoms, and for common weals,

---

19. thought] *Q 2;* taught *Q 1, Q 3.*   41. as one for] *Q 2;* for one as *Q 1,*
30. poisonous] *Q 1–2;* poysons *Q 3.*   *Q 3.*
34. our] *Q 2;* your *Q 1, Q 3.*   43. our . . . our] *Q 2;* their . . . their
38. in] *Q 2;* no *Q 1, Q 3.*   *Q 1, Q 3.*

---

29. *wry*] dissembling.
30. *wise*] ways.
42. *Sith*] since.
42. *egal*] equal.   48. *weals*] welfares.

Gave me two sons in my more lusty age
Who now in my decaying years are grown　　　　50
Well towards riper state of mind and strength
To take in hand some greater princely charge.
As yet they live and spend their hopeful days
With me and with their mother here in court.
Their age now asketh other place and trade,　　　55
And mine also doth ask another change;
Theirs to more travail, mine to greater ease.
When fatal death shall end my mortal life,
My purpose is to leave unto them twain
The realm divided in two sundry parts.　　　　60
The one, Ferrex, mine elder son, shall have;
The other shall the younger, Porrex, rule.
That both my purpose may more firmly stand
And eke that they may better rule their charge,
I mean forthwith to place them in the same,　　　65
That in my life they may both learn to rule
And I may joy to see their ruling well.
This is, in sum, what I would have ye weigh:
First, whether ye allow my whole device
And think it good for me, for them, for you,　　　70
And for our country, mother of us all.
And if ye like it and allow it well,
Then, for their guiding and their governance,
Show forth such means of circumstance
As ye think meet to be both known and kept.　　　75
Lo, this is all; now tell me your advice.

AROSTUS.

And this is much and asketh great advice;
But for my part, my sovereign lord and king,
This do I think: your majesty doth know

50. decaying] *Q 2;* deceyuynge *Q 1;*
deceiuing *Q 3.*
53. their] *Q 1, Q 3; not in Q 2.*
59. unto] *Q 1–2;* betweene *Q 3.*

60. in] *Dodsley;* into *Q 1–3.*
62. younger] *Q 2;* other *Q 1, Q 3.*
63. firmly] *Q 2–3;* framelie *Q 1.*
68. ye] *Q 1–2;* you *Q 3.*

55. *trade*] occupation.
69. *allow . . . device*] approve my whole plan.
74.] Manly suggests the insertion of "to me" or "I pray" after *forth* to
restore the meter.

How under you, in justice and in peace,   80
Great wealth and honor long we have enjoyed,
So as we cannot seem with greedy minds
To wish for change of prince or governance.
But if we like your purpose and devise,
Our liking must be deemed to proceed   85
Of rightful reason and of heedful care
Not for ourselves, but for the common state,
Sith our own state doth need no better change.
I think in all as erst your grace hath said:
First, when you shall unload your aged mind   90
Of heavy care and troubles manifold
And lay the same upon my lords, your sons,
Whose growing years may bear the burden long
(And long I pray the gods to grant it so),
And in your life, while you shall so behold   95
Their rule, their virtues, and their noble deeds
Such as their kind behighteth to us all,
Great be the profits that shall grow thereof.
Your age in quiet shall the longer last;
Your lasting age shall be their longer stay.   100
For cares of kings that rule as you have ruled,
For public wealth and not for private joy,
Do waste man's life and hasten crooked age,
With furrowed face and with enfeebled limbs,
To draw on creeping death a swifter pace.   105
They two, yet young, shall bear the parted reign
With greater ease than one, now old, alone
Can wield the whole, for whom much harder is
With lessened strength the double weight to bear.
Your eye, your counsel, and the grave regard   110
Of father, yea, of such a father's name,

84. we] *Q 2;* ye *Q 1, Q 3.*   111. father] *Q 2;* Fathers *Q 1, Q 3;*
87. the] *Q 2;* our *Q 1, Q 3.*   father's *Dodsley.*
106. parted] *Q 2;* partie *Q 1, Q 3.*

---

84. *like*] be agreeable to, approve.
88. *no better change*] no change to better it.
97. *kind behighteth*] nature promises.
100. *stay*] support, prop.
102. *wealth*] weal, well-being.   106. *parted*] divided, shared.

Now at beginning of their sundered reign
When is the hazard of their whole success,
Shall bridle so their force of youthful heats
And so restrain the rage of insolence,   115
Which most assails the young and noble minds,
And so shall guide and train in tempered stay
Their yet green bending wits with reverent awe.
As now inured with virtues at the first,
Custom, O king, shall bring delightfulness;   120
By use of virtue, vice shall grow in hate.
But if you so dispose it that the day
Which ends your life shall first begin their reign,
Great is the peril what will be the end
When such beginning of such liberties,   125
Void of such stays as in your life do lie,
Shall leave them free to randon of their will,
An open prey to traitorous flattery,
The greatest pestilence of noble youth;
Which peril shall be past, if in your life   130
Their tempered youth with aged father's awe
Be brought in ure of skilful stayedness.
And in your life, their lives disposed so
Shall length your noble life in joyfulness.
Thus think I that your grace hath wisely thought   135
And that your tender care of common weal
Hath bred this thought, so to divide your land
And plant your sons to bear the present rule
While you yet live to see their ruling well

113. is the] *Q 2;* it is *Q 1, Q 3.*   126. stays] *Q 2;* states *Q 1, Q 3.*
119. As] *Q 2;* And *Q 1, Q 3.*   127. free to] *Q 2;* to free *Q 1, Q 3.*
123. their] *Q 1–2;* the *Q 3.*   127. randon] *Q 1–2;* random *Q 3.*
124. will] *Q 1–2;* shall *Q 3.*

115. *rage of insolence*] outbreak of arrogance or disrespect of authority.
119. *inured*] habituated.
120. *Custom . . . delightfulness*] proverbial; see Tilley, C 933.
127. *to randon . . . will*] "to stray in a wild manner" (Nares).
132. *ure*] use.
132. *stayedness*] gravity, firmness; Miss Smith paraphrases lines 130–132 as "There will be no danger if, during your life, their youth, tempered by awe of you, be inured to reasonable firmness."

That you may longer live by joy therein.   140
What further means behooveful are and meet
At greater leisure may your grace devise
When all have said and when we be agreed
If this be best, to part the realm in twain
And place your sons in present government;   145
Whereof, as I have plainly said my mind,
So would I hear the rest of all my lords.

PHILANDER.

In part I think as hath been said before;
In part, again, my mind is otherwise.
As for dividing of this realm in twain   150
And lotting out the same in egal parts
To either of my lords, your grace's sons,
That think I best for this your realm's behoof,
For profit and advancement of your sons,
And for your comfort and your honor eke.   155
But so to place them while your life do last,
To yield to them your royal governance,
To be above them only in the name
Of father, not in kingly state also,
I think not good for you, for them, nor us.   160
This kingdom, since the bloody civil field
Where Morgan slain did yield his conquered part
Unto his cousin's sword in Camberland,
Containeth all that whilom did suffice
Three noble sons of your forefather Brute;   165

142. greater] *Q 2–3;* great *Q 1.*   163. Camberland] *Q 1–2;* Cumber-
148. hath] *Q 2–3;* haue *Q 1.*   land *Q 3.*
156. do] *Q 1–2;* doth *Q 3.*

---

162. *Morgan*] Morgan and Cunedag, nephews of Cordelia, took possession of the kingdom "in high dudgeon that Britain should be subject to
the rule of a woman"; after a successful rebellion, they divided the kingdom
between themselves and put Cordelia in prison. There she committed
suicide. By listening to foolish advisers, Morgan, as the elder, tried to gain
control of the whole island, but in his attempt he was slain. His victorious
cousin Cunedag governed the united kingdoms for three and thirty years
(Geoffrey of Monmouth, II.xv).

165. *Brute*] Brutus, great-grandson of Aeneas and the mythical founder of
Britain, divided the kingdom among his three sons; see the note on *Logris*
under "The Names of the Speakers."

So your two sons it may suffice also,
The moe the stronger, if they 'gree in one.
The smaller compass that the realm doth hold,
The easier is the sway thereof to weld,
The nearer justice to the wronged poor,   170
The smaller charge, and yet enough for one.
And when the region is divided so
That brethren be the lords of either part,
Such strength doth nature knit between them both,
In sundry bodies by conjoined love,   175
That, not as two, but one of doubled force,
Each is to other as a sure defense.
The nobleness and glory of the one
Doth sharp the courage of the other's mind
With virtuous envy to contend for praise.   180
And such an egalness hath nature made
Between the brethren of one father's seed
As an unkindly wrong it seems to be
To throw the brother subject under feet
Of him whose peer he is by course of kind.   185
And nature, that did make this egalness,
Oft so repineth at so great a wrong
That oft she raiseth up a grudging grief
In younger brethren at the elder's state,
Whereby both towns and kingdoms have been razed   190
And famous stocks of royal blood destroyed.
The brother, that should be the brother's aid
And have a wakeful care for his defense,
Gapes for his death and blames the lingering years
That draw not forth his end with faster course;   195
And oft impatient of so long delays,

---

166. suffice also] *Q 2;* also suffise   187. so repineth] *Q 1–2;* sore pineth
Q 1, Q 3.   *Q 3.*
174. them] *Q 2–3;* the *Q 1.*   195. draw] *Q 2;* brings *Q 1, Q 3;*
184. brother] *Q 2;* other *Q 1, Q 3.*   bring *Dodsley.*

---

167. *moe*] more.
169. *weld*] wield.
179. *sharp the courage*] sharpen the vigor.

With hateful slaughter he prevents the fates
And heaps a just reward for brother's blood
With endless vengeance on his stock for aye.
Such mischiefs here are wisely met withal,   200
If egal state may nourish egal love,
Where none hath cause to grudge at other's good.
But now the head to stoop beneath them both,
Ne kind, ne reason, ne good order bears.
And oft it hath been seen where nature's course   205
Hath been perverted in disordered wise,
When fathers cease to know that they should rule,
The children cease to know they should obey.
And often overkindly tenderness
Is mother of unkindly stubbornness.   210
I speak not this in envy or reproach,
As if I grudged the glory of your sons,
Whose honor I beseech the gods increase;
Nor yet as if I thought there did remain
So filthy cankers in their noble breasts,   215
Whom I esteem (which is their greatest praise)
Undoubted children of so good a king.
Only I mean to show, by certain rules
Which kind hath graft within the mind of man,
That nature hath her order and her course,   220
Which (being broken) doth corrupt the state
Of minds and things, even in the best of all.
My lords, your sons, may learn to rule of you:
Your own example in your noble court
Is fittest guider of their youthful years.   225
If you desire to see some present joy

197. prevents] *Q 2;* presentes *Q 1;*
presents *Q 3.*
198. heaps] *Q 2;* keepes *Q 1, Q 3.*
205. where nature's course] *Q 2;*
that where Nature *Q 1, Q 3.*
208. The] *Q 2;* And *Q 1, Q 3.*

209. overkindly] *Q 2;* our vnkindly
Q 1, Q 3.
213. increase] *Q 2;* to encrease *Q 1;*
to in-crease *Q 3.*
218. by] *Q 2;* my *Q 1, Q 3.*
226. see] *Q 2;* seeke *Q 1, Q 3.*

197. *prevents*] anticipates.
204. *Ne*] neither, nor.
209. *overkindly tenderness*] tenderness beyond the normal.
219. *kind*] natural or basic sense.
220. *nature . . . course*] proverbial; see Tilley, N 48.

By sight of their well ruling in your life,
See them obey; so shall you see them rule.
Whoso obeyeth not with humbleness
Will rule with outrage and with insolence.   230
Long may they rule I do beseech the gods;
Long may they learn ere they begin to rule.
If kind and fates would suffer, I would wish
Them aged princes and immortal kings.
Wherefore, most noble king, I well assent   235
Between your sons that you divide your realm;
And as in kind, so match them in degree.
But while the gods prolong your royal life,
Prolong your reign; for thereto live you here,
And therefore have the gods so long forborne   240
To join you to themselves that still you might
Be prince and father of our common weal.
They, when they see your children ripe to rule,
Will make them room and will remove you hence
That yours, in right ensuing of your life,   245
May rightly honor your immortal name.

EUBULUS.

Your wonted true regard of faithful hearts
Makes me, O king, the bolder to presume
To speak what I conceive within my breast,
Although the same do not agree at all   250
With that which other here my lords have said
Nor which yourself have seemed best to like.
Pardon I crave, and that my words be deemed
To flow from hearty zeal unto your grace
And to the safety of your common weal.   255
To part your realm unto my lords, your sons,
I think not good for you, ne yet for them,
But worst of all for this our native land.

---

230. with outrage] *Q 2–3;* without
rage *Q 1.*
232. Long] *Sackville-West, Manly;*
But long *Q 1–3.*

233. fates] *Q 1–2;* saies *Q 3.*
235. well] *Q 1–2;* will *Q 3.*
246. immortal] *Q 2;* mortall *Q 1,*
Q 3.

232.] Sackville-West regularized this line by omitting the quartos' *But;*
Manly noted that the first *they* could as well have been omitted.
   233. *suffer*] allow.

Within one land one single rule is best:
Divided reigns do make divided hearts,   260
But peace preserves the country and the prince.
Such is in man the greedy mind to reign,
So great is his desire to climb aloft,
In worldly stage the stateliest parts to bear,
That faith and justice and all kindly love   265
Do yield unto desire of sovereignty,
Where egal state doth raise an egal hope
To win the thing that either would attain.
Your grace rememb'reth how in passed years
The mighty Brute, first prince of all this land,   270
Possessed the same and ruled it well in one;
He, thinking that the compass did suffice
For his three sons three kingdoms eke to make,
Cut it in three, as you would now in twain.
But how much British blood hath since been spilt   275
To join again the sundered unity!
What princes slain before their timely hour!
What waste of towns and people in the land!
What treasons heaped on murders and on spoils!
Whose just revenge even yet is scarcely ceased;   280
Ruthful remembrance is yet raw in mind.
The gods forbid the like to chance again.
And you, O king, give not the cause thereof.
My lord Ferrex, your elder son, perhaps,
Whom kind and custom gives a rightful hope   285
To be your heir and to succeed your reign,
Shall think that he doth suffer greater wrong
Than he perchance will bear, if power serve.
Porrex, the younger, so upraised in state,
Perhaps in courage will be raised also.   290

259. Within] *Q 2;* For with *Q 1,*
Q 3.
260. reigns] *Q 1–2;* Regions *Q 3.*
275. British] *Q 2;* Brutish *Q 1, Q 3.*
275. since] *Q 2;* sithence *Q 1, Q 3.*

277. hour] *Q 2;* honour *Q 1, Q 3.*
281. raw] *Q 2;* had *Q 1, Q 3.*
289. upraised] *Q 2;* vnpaised *Q 1,*
Q 3.

270–274.] See above, l. 165, note.
272. *compass*] extent.
290. *courage*] ambition or aspiration.

If flattery then, which fails not to assail
The tender minds of yet unskilful youth,
In one shall kindle and increase disdain
And envy in the other's heart inflame,
This fire shall waste their love, their lives, their land,   295
And ruthful ruin shall destroy them both.
I wish not this, O king, so to befall,
But fear the thing that I do most abhor.
Give no beginning to so dreadful end.
Keep them in order and obedience;   300
And let them both by now obeying you
Learn such behavior as beseems their state:
The elder, mildness in his governance,
The younger, a yielding contentedness.
And keep them near unto your presence still   305
That they, restrained by the awe of you,
May live in compass of well tempered stay
And pass the perils of their youthful years.
Your aged life draws on to feebler time
Wherein you shall less able be to bear   310
The travails that in youth you have sustained,
Both in your person's and your realm's defense.
If planting now your sons in further parts,
You send them further from your present reach,
Less shall you know how they themselves demean.   315
Traitorous corrupters of their pliant youth
Shall have unspied a much more free access;
And if ambition and inflamed disdain
Shall arm the one, the other, or them both
To civil war or to usurping pride,   320
Late shall you rue that you ne recked before.
Good is, I grant, of all to hope the best,

294. And] *Q 1–2;* In *Q 3.*   *Q 3.*
315. demean] *Q 2;* demaund *Q 1,*   318. if] *Q 2;* of *Q 1, Q 3.*

292. *unskilful*] lacking in knowledge.
296. *ruthful*] pitiful.
302. *beseems*] befits.
307. *in . . . stay*] within the bounds of moderation.
315. *themselves demean*] conduct themselves.
321. *recked*] heeded.

But not to live still dreadless of the worst.
So trust the one that the other be foreseen.
Arm not unskilfulness with princely power.   325
But you, that long have wisely ruled the reins
Of royalty within your noble realm,
So hold them, while the gods for our avails
Shall stretch the thread of your prolonged days.
Too soon he clamb into the flaming car   330
Whose want of skill did set the earth on fire.
Time and example of your noble grace
Shall teach your sons both to obey and rule.
When time hath taught them, time shall make them place,
The place that now is full; and so I pray   335
Long it remain, to comfort of us all.

GORBODUC.

I take your faithful hearts in thankful part;
But sith I see no cause to draw my mind
To fear the nature of my loving sons,
Or to misdeem that envy or disdain   340
Can there work hate where nature planteth love,
In one self purpose do I still abide.
My love extendeth egally to both,
My land sufficeth for them both also.
Humber shall part the marches of their realms.   345
The southern part the elder shall possess;
The northern shall Porrex, the younger, rule.
In quiet I will pass mine aged days,

330. car] *Q 2;* carte *Q 1, Q 3.*   334. place] *Q 2;* pace *Q 1, Q 3;*
                                             space *Dodsley.*

---

326. *reins*] "There is here a play on the word *reins,* in the sense of guiding
them *(rego)* or holding in *(retineo)*" (Smith).

328. *avails*] profit.

330. *he*] Phaeton, Apollo's inconsiderate and ambitious son, who
foolishly insisted on driving the sun-chariot for one day. His fall symbolized
"ambition for power to rule or, given the power, inability to handle the
'unruly jades'" (Starnes and Talbot). There are other references to Phaeton
in I.ii. 385–387 and II.i.204.

330. *clamb*] climbed.

338. *draw*] influence.

342. *self*] sole.

345. *marches*] boundaries.

Free from the travail and the painful cares
That hasten age upon the worthiest kings.   350
But, lest the fraud that ye do seem to fear
Of flattering tongues corrupt their tender youth
And writhe them to the ways of youthful lust,
To climbing pride or to revenging hate,
Or to neglecting of their careful charge   355
Lewdly to live in wanton recklessness,
Or to oppressing of the rightful cause,
Or not to wreak the wrongs done to the poor,
To tread down truth or favor false deceit,
I mean to join to either of my sons   360
Some one of those whose long approved faith
And wisdom tried may well assure my heart
That mining fraud shall find no way to creep
Into their fenced ears with grave advice.
This is the end, and so I pray you all   365
To bear my sons the love and loyalty
That I have found within your faithful breasts.

AROSTUS.

You, nor your sons, our sovereign lord, shall want
Our faith and service while our lives do last.   [*Exeunt.*]

CHORUS.

When settled stay doth hold the royal throne   370
    In steadfast place, by known and doubtless right,
And chiefly when descent on one alone
    Makes single and unparted reign to light,
Each change of course unjoints the whole estate
    And yields it thrall to ruin by debate.   375

353. writhe] *Q 2;* wrieth *Q 1, Q 3.*   *other Choruses (Acts II, III, IV] follow*
wrie *Dodsley.*   *Q 1's form.*
370.] *Q 2 does not arrange Chorus in*   373. Makes] *Q 2;* Make *Q 1, Q 3.*
stanzaic pattern; printed here as in Q 1;

353. *writhe*] twist, divert.
353. *lust*] ambition.
356. *Lewdly*] basely.
358. *wreak*] avenge.
363. *mining*] undermining.
364. *fenced . . . advice*] i.e., ears fortified with grave advice.
368. *want*] lack.
375. *debate*] dissension.

The strength that, knit by fast accord in one
   Against all foreign power of mighty foes,
Could of itself defend itself alone,
   Disjoined once, the former force doth lose.
The sticks that sundered brake so soon in twain   380
   In fagot bound attempted were in vain.

Oft tender mind that leads the partial eye
   Of erring parents in their children's love
Destroys the wrongly loved child thereby.
   This doth the proud son of Apollo prove   385
Who, rashly set in chariot of his sire,
   Inflamed the parched earth with heaven's fire.

And this great king, that doth divide his land
   And change the course of his descending crown
And yields the reign into his children's hand,   390
   From blissful state of joy and great renown,
A mirror shall become to princes all
   To learn to shun the cause of such a fall.

The Order and Signification of the Dumb Show
Before the Second Act

First, the music of cornets began to play, during which
came in upon the stage a king accompanied with a number
of his nobility and gentlemen. And after he had placed himself in a chair of estate prepared for him, there came and
kneeled before him a grave and aged gentleman and offered   5
up a cup unto him of wine in a glass, which the king refused.
After him comes a brave and lusty young gentleman and

376. fast] *Q 2;* laste *Q 1;* last *Q 3.*   389. change] *Q 2;* chaunged *Q 1;*
384. wrongly] *Q 2;* wrongfull *Q 1,*   chaungde *Q 3.*
Q 3.   [Dumb Show]
                                 6. the] *Q 1, Q 3;* the the *Q 2.*

---

382. *partial*] biased, prejudiced.
385. *proud son*] Phaeton.
389. *descending*] hereditary.
392. *mirror*] show, exemplar.
[Dumb Show]
   7. *lusty*] vigorous.

presents the king with a cup of gold filled with poison, which
the king accepted, and drinking the same, immediately fell
down dead upon the stage, and so was carried thence away   10
by his lords and gentlemen, and then the music ceased.
Hereby was signified, that as glass by nature holdeth no
poison, but is clear and may easily be seen through, ne
boweth by any art; so a faithful counselor holdeth no
treason, but is plain and open, ne yieldeth to any undiscreet   15
affection, but giveth wholesome counsel, which the ill-
advised prince refuseth. The delightful gold filled with
poison betokeneth flattery, which under fair seeming of
pleasant words beareth deadly poison, which destroyed the
prince that receiveth it. As befell in the two brethren,   20
Ferrex and Porrex, who, refusing the wholesome advice of
grave counselors, credited these young parasites and brought
to themselves death and destruction thereby.

[II.i]   [*Enter*] Ferrex, Hermon, [*and*] Dordan.

FERREX.

    I marvel much what reason led the king,
    My father, thus, without all my desert,
    To reave me half the kingdom which by course
    Of law and nature should remain to me.

HERMON.

    If you with stubborn and untamed pride   5
    Had stood against him in rebelling wise,
    Or if with grudging mind you had envied

8. of] *Q 1, Q 3; not in Q 2.*
10. the] *Q 1, Q 3;* the the *Q 2.*
16. giveth] *Q 1–2;* giueth any *Q 3.*
19. destroyed] *Q 2;* destroieth *Q 1,*
Q 3.

23. to] *Q 1–2;* vnto *Q 3.*
[II.i]
6. rebelling] *Q 2;* rebellious *Q 1,*
Q 3.

---

   8. *poison*] "To drink poison from golden cups" was commonplace; see
Tilley, P 458. The audience would know, too, that one cannot trust in
appearances.
   14. *boweth*] yields, submits.
   15. *undiscreet*] indiscreet.
   22. *credited*] believed, trusted.
[II.i]
   3. *reave me*] rob me by violence of.

So slow a sliding of his aged years,
Or sought before your time to haste the course
Of fatal death upon his royal head,   10
Or stained your stock with murder of your kin,
Some face of reason might perhaps have seemed
To yield some likely cause to spoil ye thus.

FERREX.

The wreakful gods pour on my cursed head
Eternal plagues and never-dying woes,   15
The hellish prince adjudge my damned ghost
To Tantale's thirst, or proud Ixion's wheel,
Or cruel gripe to gnaw my growing heart,
To during torments and unquenched flames,
If ever I conceived so foul a thought,   20
To wish his end of life or yet of reign.

DORDAN.

Ne yet your father, O most noble prince,
Did ever think so foul a thing of you.
For he, with more than father's tender love,

17. Tantale's] *Q 2;* Tantalus *Q 1,*   18. growing] *Q 1–2;* groaning *Q 3.*
Q 3.

---

8. *sliding*] passing.
14. *wreakful*] avenging.
16–17. *The . . . wheel*] The hellish prince, Hades, had as lodgers in Hell,
among others, Tantalus and Ixion. Tantalus, proud of his association with
the gods, invited them to a feast for which his son Pelops had been prepared
as the main dish to prove that the gods could not tell human flesh from
animal. They could. For his impiety, he was sentenced to an eternity of
standing up to his neck in water that recedes when he tries to drink;
above him were branches of savory fruit that were blown out of his reach
when he tried to eat. Ixion, who promised rich gifts for his marriage,
killed his father-in-law to escape his obligations. Because no earthly means
could purify him, Zeus carried him to Olympus where Ixion tried to seduce
Hera. Zeus made a phantom Hera, and Ixion sired by her the race of
centaurs. As further punishment, Ixion was banished to Hades and tied to
a fiery wheel that endlessly turned.
18. *gripe*] griffin or vulture; the allusion here may be to the punishment
of Tityus who, having attempted to ravish Latona, his sister, was hurled
into Hades where vultures eternally ate his liver which was constantly
renewed (Starnes and Talbot). Cf., also, the punishment of Prometheus.
18. *growing*] Q3's *groaning* is probably a sophistication for *growing*, "to
increase in size, quantity, or degree."
19. *during*] enduring.

While yet the Fates do lend him life to rule   25
(Who long might live to see your ruling well),
To you, my lord, and to his other son,
Lo, he resigns his realm and royalty;
Which never would so wise a prince have done
If he had once misdeemed that in your heart   30
There ever lodged so unkind a thought.
But tender love, my lord, and settled trust
Of your good nature and your noble mind
Made him to place you thus in royal throne
And now to give you half his realm to guide;   35
Yea, and that half which in abounding store
Of things that serve to make a wealthy realm,
In stately cities and in fruitful soil,
In temperate breathing of the milder heaven,
In things of needful use which friendly sea   40
Transports by traffic from the foreign parts,
In flowing wealth, in honor, and in force,
Doth pass the double value of the part
That Porrex hath alloted to his reign.
Such is your case, such is your father's love.   45

FERREX.

Ah love, my friends? Love wrongs not whom he loves.

DORDAN.

Ne yet he wrongeth you that giveth you
So large a reign ere that the course of time
Bring you to kingdom by descended right,
Which time perhaps might end your time before.   50

FERREX.

Is this no wrong, say you, to reave from me
My native right of half so great a realm?
And thus to match his younger son with me
In egal power and in as great degree?
Yea, and what son? The son whose swelling pride   55

36. which in] *Q 2;* within *Q 1, Q 3.*   41. parts] *Q 2;* Portes *Q 1, Q 3.*

---

30. *misdeemed*] suspected.

43. *pass*] surpass.

50. *Which . . . before*] "Your life might end before the time you would
inherit the kingdom."

Would never yield one point of reverence
When I, the elder and apparent heir,
Stood in the likelihood to possess the whole;
Yea, and that son which from his childish age
Envieth mine honor and doth hate my life.   60
What will he now do, when his pride, his rage,
The mindful malice of his grudging heart
Is armed with force, with wealth, and kingly state?

HERMON.

Was this not wrong, yea, ill-advised wrong,
To give so mad a man so sharp a sword,   65
To so great peril of so great mishap,
Wide open thus to set so large a way?

DORDAN.

Alas, my lord, what grieffull thing is this,
That of your brother you can think so ill?
I never saw him utter likely sign   70
Whereby a man might see or once misdeem
Such hate of you ne such unyielding pride.
Ill is their counsel, shameful be their end,
That raising such mistrustful fear in you,
Sowing the seed of such unkindly hate,   75
Travail by treason to destroy you both.
Wise is your brother and of noble hope,
Worthy to wield a large and mighty realm.
So much a stronger friend have you thereby,
Whose strength is your strength if you 'gree in one.   80

HERMON.

If nature and the gods had pinched so
Their flowing bounty and their noble gifts
Of princely qualities from you, my lord,
And poured them all at once in wasteful wise
Upon your father's younger son alone,   85
Perhaps there be that in your prejudice

76. treason] *Q 2;* reason *Q 1, Q 3.*

---

62. *mindful malice*] "unforgetful ill-will" (Smith).
80. *'gree in one*] agree together.
81. *pinched*] stinted.
86. *in . . . prejudice*] to your damage.

−29−

Would say that birth should yield to worthiness.
But sith in each good gift and princely art
Ye are his match, and in the chief of all,
In mildness and in sober governance,   90
Ye far surmount; and sith there is in you
Sufficing skill and hopeful towardness
To weld the whole and match your elder's praise,
I see no cause why ye should lose the half,
Ne would I wish you yield to such a loss,   95
Lest your mild sufferance of so great a wrong
Be deemed cowardice and simple dread,
Which shall give courage to the fiery head
Of your young brother to invade the whole.
While yet therefore sticks in the people's mind   100
The loathed wrong of your disheritance;
And ere your brother have by settled power,
By guileful cloak of an alluring show,
Got him some force and favor in the realm;
And while the noble queen, your mother, lives,   105
To work and practice all for your avail;
Attempt redress by arms and wreak yourself
Upon his life that gaineth by your loss,
Who now, to shame of you and grief of us,
In your own kingdom triumphs over you.   110
Show now your courage meet for kingly state,
That they which have avowed to spend their goods,
Their lands, their lives, and honors in your cause
May be the bolder to maintain your part,
When they do see that coward fear in you   115
Shall not betray ne fail their faithful hearts.
If once the death of Porrex end the strife
And pay the price of his usurped reign,

88. art] *Q 2;* Acte *Q 1, Q 3.*   100. While] *Q 2;* Whiles *Q 1, Q 3.*
97. cowardice]   cowardise   *Q 3;*   104. the] *Q 2;* this *Q 1, Q 3.*
cowardishe *Q 1–2.*   111. state] *Q 2;* estate *Q 1, Q 3.*

106. *practice*] plot.
111. *meet*] proper.
112. *avowed*] promised on oath.
116. *fail*] "to beguile, delude (Lat. *fallere*)" (Smith).

Your mother shall persuade the angry king.
The lords, your friends, eke shall appease his rage.   120
For they be wise, and well they can foresee
That ere long time your aged father's death
Will bring a time when you shall well requite
Their friendly favor or their hateful spite,
Yea, or their slackness to advance your cause.   125
"Wise men do not so hang on passing state
Of present princes, chiefly in their age,
But they will further cast their reaching eye,
To view and weigh the times and reigns to come."
Ne is it likely, though the king be wroth,   130
That he yet will or that the realm will bear
Extreme revenge upon his only son;
Or, if he would, what one is he that dare
Be minister to such an enterprise?
And here you be now placed in your own   135
Amid your friends, your vassals, and your strength.
We shall defend and keep your person safe
Till either counsel turn his tender mind
Or age or sorrow end his weary days.
But if the fear of gods and secret grudge   140
Of nature's law, repining at the fact,
Withhold your courage from so great attempt,
Know ye that lust of kingdoms hath no law.
The gods do bear and well allow in kings
The things that they abhor in rascal routs.   145
"When kings on slender quarrels run to wars,
And then in cruel and unkindly wise

---

145. that] *Dodsley; not in* Q 1–3.

---

119. *persuade*] win over, reconcile.
126–129.] The quotation marks are used in the play to set off sententious remarks; see also II.i.146–151.
138. *tender*] pliant.
140. *grudge*] misgiving.
141. *repining . . . fact*] "Nature turns with pain, or shrinks, from the deed of killing a brother" (Smith).
143. *lust . . . law*] An excessive desire to rule has no bounds; the saying is proverbial (cf. Tilley, K 90). Cunliffe cites Seneca's *Agamemnon*, ll. 264, 268–272.
145. *rascal routs*] the rabble.

Command thefts, rapes, murders of innocents,
The spoil of towns, ruins of mighty realms;
Think you such princes do suppose themselves   150
Subject to laws of kind and fear of gods?"
Murders and violent thefts in private men
Are heinous crimes and full of foul reproach;
Yet none offense, but decked with glorious name
Of noble conquests in the hands of kings.   155
But if you like not yet so hot devise
Ne list to take such vantage of the time,
But, though with peril of your own estate,
You will not be the first that shall invade,
Assemble yet your force for your defense   160
And for your safety stand upon your guard.

DORDAN.

O heaven! was there ever heard or known
So wicked counsel to a noble prince?
Let me, my lord, disclose unto your grace
This heinous tale, what mischief it contains: 165
Your father's death, your brother's, and your own,
Your present murder and eternal shame.
Hear me, O king, and suffer not to sink
So high a treason in your princely breast.

FERREX.

The mighty gods forbid that ever I   170
Should once conceive such mischief in my heart.
Although my brother hath bereft my realm
And bear perhaps to me an hateful mind,
Shall I revenge it with his death therefore?
Or shall I so destroy my father's life   175
That gave me life? The gods forbid, I say.
Cease you to speak so any more to me;

---

148. murders] *Q2;* murder *Q1,*
Q3.
149. The] *Q2;* To *Q1, Q3.*
149. ruins]*Q2;* & reignes *Q1, Q3.*
150. suppose] *Q2;* suppresse *Q1,*
Q3.

154–155.] *placed before ll. 152–153 in*
Q1, Q3.
158. with] *Q2;* with great *Q1, Q3.*
158. own estate] *Q2;* state *Q1, Q3.*
173. an] *Q2–3;* and *Q1.*

---

156. *devise*] scheme, plan.

Ne you, my friend, with answer once repeat
So foul a tale. In silence let it die.
What lord or subject shall have hope at all   180
That under me they safely shall enjoy
Their goods, their honors, lands, and liberties,
With whom neither one only brother dear,
Ne father dearer, could enjoy their lives?
But, sith I fear my younger brother's rage,   185
And sith, perhaps, some other man may give
Some like advice, to move his grudging head
At mine estate—which counsel may perchance
Take greater force with him than this with me—
I will in secret so prepare myself,   190
As if his malice or his lust to reign
Break forth in arms or sudden violence,
I may withstand his rage and keep mine own.

> [*Exeunt* Ferrex *and* Hermon.]

DORDAN.

I fear the fatal time now draweth on
When civil hate shall end the noble line   195
Of famous Brute and of his royal seed.
Great Jove, defend the mischiefs now at hand!
O that the Secretary's wise advice
Had erst been heard when he besought the king
Not to divide his land, nor send his sons   200
To further parts from presence of his court,
Ne yet to yield to them his governance.
Lo, such are they now in the royal throne
As was rash Phaeton in Phoebus' car;
Ne then the fiery steeds did draw the flame   205
With wilder randon through the kindled skies
Than traitorous counsel now will whirl about
The youthful heads of these unskilful kings.
But I hereof their father will inform;

---

192. in] *Q 2;* with *Q 1, Q 3.*   204. rash] *Q 1–2;* that *Q 3.*

---

191. *As if*] so that if.
197. *defend*] ward off.
198. *Secretary*] Eubulus (see I.ii.247 ff.).
206. *randon*] a random course (*OED*).

The reverence of him perhaps shall stay   210
The growing mischiefs while they yet are green.
If this help not, then woe unto themselves,
The prince, the people, the divided land.   [*Exit.*]

[II.ii]   [*Enter*] Porrex, Tyndar, [*and*] Philander.

PORREX.

And is it thus? And doth he so prepare
Against his brother as his mortal foe?
And now, while yet his aged father lives?
Neither regards he him nor fears he me?
War would he have? And he shall have it so!   5

TYNDAR.

I saw, myself, the great prepared store
Of horse, of armor, and of weapons there;
Ne bring I to my lord reported tales
Without the ground of seen and searched truth.
Lo, secret quarrels run about his court   10
To bring the name of you, my lord, in hate.
Each man almost can now debate the cause
And ask a reason of so great a wrong,
Why he, so noble and so wise a prince,
Is, as unworthy, reft his heritage,   15
And why the king, misled by crafty means,
Divided thus his land from course of right.
The wiser sort hold down their griefful heads;
Each man withdraws from talk and company
Of those that have been known to favor you.   20
To hide the mischief of their meaning there,
Rumors are spread of your preparing here.
The rascal numbers of unskilful sort
Are filled with monstrous tales of you and yours.
In secret I was counseled by my friends   25
To haste me thence and brought you, as you know,
Letters from those that both can truly tell
And would not write unless they knew it well.

7. armor] *Q 2;* Armours *Q 1, Q 3.*   14. Why] *Q 2;* While *Q 1, Q 3.*
7. weapons] *Q 1, Q 3;* weapon *Q 2.*   23. of] *Q 2;* of the *Q 1, Q 3.*

PHILANDER.

My lord, yet ere you move unkindly war,
Send to your brother to demand the cause.   30
Perhaps some traitorous tales have filled his ears
With false reports against your noble grace;
Which, once disclosed, shall end the growing strife
That else, not stayed with wise foresight in time,
Shall hazard both your kingdoms and your lives.   35
Send to your father eke; he shall appease
Your kindled minds and rid you of this fear.

PORREX.

Rid me of fear! I fear him not at all;
Ne will to him ne to my father send.
If danger were for one to tarry there,   40
Think ye it safety to return again?
In mischiefs, such as Ferrex now intends,
The wonted courteous laws to messengers
Are not observed, which in just war they use.
Shall I so hazard any one of mine?   45
Shall I betray my trusty friends to him,
That have disclosed his treason unto me?
Let him entreat that fears; I fear him not.
Or shall I to the king, my father, send?
Yea, and send now, while such a mother lives   50
That loves my brother and that hateth me?
Shall I give leisure, by my fond delays,
To Ferrex to oppress me all unware?
I will not; but I will invade his realm
And seek the traitor prince within his court.   55
Mischief for mischief is a due reward.

29. move] *Q 2;* nowe *Q 1;* now *Q 3.*   *Q 3.*
41. safety] *Q 2;* safely *Q 1, Q 3.*   47. have] *Q 2;* hath *Q 1, Q 3.*
46. friends] *Q 2;* friende *Q 1;* frend   53. all] *Q 2;* at *Q 1, Q 3.*

40. *If danger were*] if it was dangerous.
52. *fond*] foolish.
53. *oppress*] overpower, overwhelm.
56. *Mischief . . . reward*] proverbial; see Tilley, C 826. A line from Seneca's
Agamemnon (Studley's translation) is "The safest path to mischief is by
mischief open still" (Herrick).

His wretched head shall pay the worthy price
Of this his treason and his hate to me.
Shall I abide and treat and send and pray
And hold my yielden throat to traitor's knife,   60
While I, with valiant mind and conquering force,
Might rid myself of foes and win a realm?
Yet rather, when I have the wretch's head,
Then to the king, my father, will I send.
The bootless case may yet appease his wrath;   65
If not, I will defend me as I may.

[*Exeunt* Porrex *and* Tyndar.]

PHILANDER.

Lo, here the end of these two youthful kings,
The father's death, the ruin of their realms!
"O most unhappy state of counselors,
That light on so unhappy lords and times   70
That neither can their good advice be heard,
Yet must they bear the blames of ill success."
But I will to the king, their father, haste
Ere this mischief come to the likely end;
That, if the mindful wrath of wreakful gods   75
(Since mighty Ilion's fall not yet appeased
With these poor remnants of the Trojan name)
Have not determined by unmoved fate
Out of this realm to raze the British line;
By good advice, by awe of father's name,   80
By force of wiser lords, this kindled hate
May yet be quenched ere it consume us all.   [*Exit.*]

---

59. and treat] *Q2;* entreate *Q1;*
intreat *Q3.*
63. Yet] *Q1–3;* Yea *Dodsley.*
68. ruin of their realms] *Q2;*
reigne of their two realmes *Q1, Q3;*
ruin of their two realms *Dodsley.*
74. the] *Q2;* that *Q1, Q3.*

77. remnants] *Q2;* remnant *Q1,*
Q3.
77. Trojan] *Q2;* Troians *Q1, Q3.*
78. determined by] *Q2;* deter-
minedlie *Q1;* determinedly *Q3.*
79. British] *Q2;* Brutish *Q1, Q3.*

---

59. *treat*] entreat.
60. *yielden*] yielded.
65. *bootless case*] irremediable matter.
75. *mindful wrath*] unforgetful wrath.
76. *Ilion*] Troy.

CHORUS.

When youth not bridled with a guiding stay
    Is left to randon of their own delight
And welds whole realms by force of sovereign sway,   85
    Great is the danger of unmastered might,
Lest skilless rage throw down with headlong fall
Their lands, their states, their lives, themselves and all.

When growing pride doth fill the swelling breast
    And greedy lust doth raise the climbing mind,   90
O, hardly may the peril be repressed.
    Ne fear of angry gods, ne lawes kind,
Ne country's care can fired hearts restrain
When force hath armed envy and disdain.

When kings of foreset will neglect the rede   95
    Of best advice and yield to pleasing tales
That do their fancies' noisome humor feed,
    Ne reason nor regard of right avails.
Succeeding heaps of plagues shall teach too late
To learn the mischiefs of misguided state.   100

Foul fall the traitor false that undermines
    The love of brethren to destroy them both.
Woe to the prince that pliant ear inclines
    And yields his mind to poisonous tale that floweth
From flattering mouth! And woe to wretched land   105
That wastes itself with civil sword in hand!
    Lo, thus it is, poison in gold to take
And wholesome drink in homely cup forsake.

---

85. sway] *Q 2;* fraie *Q 1;* fray *Q 3.*
92. lawes kind] *Q 1–3;* laws of kind
Hawkins.
93. country's] *Q 2;* Countrie *Q 1;*
Country *Q 3.*
100. misguided] *Q 2;* misguydinge
Q 1; misguiding *Q 3.*

---

92. *lawes kind*] laws affecting kindred; the spelling *lawes* indicates a
dissyllable.
    95. *of foreset*] deliberately.
    95. *rede*] counsel.

The Order and Signification of the Dumb Show
Before the Third Act

  First, the music of flutes began to play, during which came
in upon the stage a company of mourners, all clad in black,
betokening death and sorrow to ensue upon the ill-advised
misgovernment and dissension of brethren, as befell upon the
murder of Ferrex by his younger brother. After the mourners 5
had passed thrice about the stage, they departed, and then
the music ceased.

[III.i]   [*Enter*] Gorboduc, Eubulus, [*and*] Arostus.

GORBODUC.

  O cruel fates, O mindful wrath of gods,
  Whose vengeance neither Simois' stained streams
  Flowing with blood of Trojan princes slain,
  Nor Phrygian fields made rank with corpses dead
  Of Asian kings and lords can yet appease;   5
  Ne slaughter of unhappy Priam's race,
  Nor Ilion's fall made level with the soil
  Can yet suffice; but still continued rage
  Pursues our lives and from the farthest seas
  Doth chase the issues of destroyed Troy.   10
  "O no man happy till his end be seen."
  If any flowing wealth and seeming joy
  In present years might make a happy wight,
  Happy was Hecuba, the woeful'st wretch
  That ever lived to make a mirror of;   15

[Dumb Show]   [III.i]
5. murder] *Q 1, Q 3;* murderer *Q 2.* 2. stained] *Q 2;* streined *Q 1, Q 3.*
7. ceased] *Q 1–2;* caused *Q 3.*   9. Pursues] *Q 2;* Persue *Q 1, Q 3.*
               9. lives] *Q 1, Q 3;* lynes *Q 2.*
               10. chase] *Q 2;* chast *Q 1, Q 3.*

[III.i]

  2. *Simois*] a river of Troy.

  4. *Phrygian*] an ancient country in Asia Minor near Troy.

  11. "*O . . . seen*"] a commonplace, reminiscent of Sophocles in the final
chorus of *Oedipus Rex* and of Herodotus; cf. Tilley, M 333.

  14. *Hecuba*] Priam's wife, Queen of Troy, a traditional figure of tragic
despair in her mourning over her slain children.

  14–15. *the . . . lived*] The description "may owe something to Chaucer's
'the wofulleste wyght that evere was' (*Troilus* IV.516–517)" (Herrick).

And happy Priam with his noble sons;
And happy I till now, alas, I see
And feel my most unhappy wretchedness.
Behold, my lords, read ye this letter here;
Lo, it contains the ruin of our realm   20
If timely speed provide not hasty help.
Yet, O ye gods, if ever woeful king
Might move ye, kings of kings, wreak it on me
And on my sons, not on this guiltless realm.
Send down your wasting flames from wrathful skies   25
To reave me and my sons the hateful breath.
Read, read, my lords; this is the matter why
I called ye now to have your good advice.

The letter from Dordan, *the counselor of the elder Prince.*

EUBULUS (*readeth the letter*).
    "My sovereign lord, what I am loath to write,
    But loathest am to see, that I am forced   30
    By letters now to make you understand.
    My lord Ferrex, your eldest son, misled
    By traitorous fraud of young untempered wits,
    Assembleth force against your younger son,
    Ne can my counsel yet withdraw the heat   35
    And furious pangs of his inflamed head.
    Disdain, saith he, of his disheritance
    Arms him to wreak the great pretended wrong
    With civil sword upon his brother's life.
    If present help do not restrain this rage,   40
    This flame will waste your sons, your land, and you.
              Your Majesty's faithful and most
                    humble subject, Dordan."
AROSTUS.
    O king, appease your grief and stay your plaint.
    Great is the matter and a woeful case,   45
    But timely knowledge may bring timely help.

20. our] *Q 1–2;* this *Q 3.*   37. disheritance] *Q 2;* inheritaunce
23. ye] *Q 2;* you *Q 1, Q 3.*   *Q 1, Q 3.*
33. traitorous fraud] *Q 2;* traitours   46. timely] *Q 1–2;* manly *Q 3.*
framde *Q 1, Q 3.*

38. *pretended*] intended.

−39−

Send for them both unto your presence here;
The reverence of your honor, age, and state,
Your grave advice, the awe of father's name
Shall quickly knit again this broken peace.   50
And if in either of my lords, your sons,
Be such untamed and unyielding pride
As will not bend unto your noble hests;
If Ferrex, the elder son, can bear no peer,
Or Porrex, not content, aspires to more   55
Than you him gave above his native right,
Join with the juster side; so shall you force
Them to agree and hold the land in stay.

EUBULUS.

What meaneth this? Lo, yonder comes in haste
Philander from my lord your younger son.   60

[*Enter* Philander.]

GORBODUC.

The gods send joyful news!

PHILANDER.   The mighty Jove
Preserve your majesty, O noble king.

GORBODUC.

Philander, welcome; but how doth my son?

PHILANDER.

Your son, sir, lives, and healthy I him left.
But yet, O king, the want of lustful health   65
Could not be half so griefful to your grace
As these most wretched tidings that I bring.

GORBODUC.

O heavens, yet more? No end of woes to me?

PHILANDER.

Tyndar, O king, came lately from the court
Of Ferrex to my lord your younger son   70
And made report of great prepared store
For war and saith that it is wholly meant
Against Porrex, for high disdain that he

48. honor, age] *Q 1, Q 3;* honourage   68. No] *Q 1, Q 3;* not *Q 2.*
Q 2.   72. For] *Q 2;* Of *Q 1, Q 3.*
65. the] *Q 2;* this *Q 1, Q 3.*

53. *hests*] behests, commands.

Lives now a king and egal in degree
With him that claimeth to succeed the whole,   75
As by due title of descending right.
Porrex is now so set on flaming fire,
Partly with kindled rage of cruel wrath,
Partly with hope to gain a realm thereby,
That he in haste prepareth to invade   80
His brother's land and with unkindly war
Threatens the murder of your elder son;
Ne could I him persuade that first he should
Send to his brother to demand the cause,
Nor yet to you to stay this hateful strife.   85
Wherefore sith there no more I can be heard,
I come myself now to inform your grace
And to beseech you, as you love the life
And safety of your children and your realm,
Now to employ your wisdom and your force   90
To stay this mischief ere it be too late.

GORBODUC.

Are they in arms? Would he not send to me?
Is this the honor of a father's name?
In vain we travail to assuage their minds,
As if their hearts, whom neither brother's love,   95
Nor father's awe, nor kingdom's cares can move,
Our counsels could withdraw from raging heat.
Jove slay them both and end the cursed line!
For though perhaps fear of such mighty force
As I, my lords, joined with your noble aids,   100
May yet raise, shall repress their present heat,
The secret grudge and malice will remain.
The fire not quenched, but kept in close restraint,
Fed still within, breaks forth with double flame.
Their death and mine must 'pease the angry gods.   105

PHILANDER.

Yield not, O king, so much to weak despair.
Your sons yet live, and long I trust they shall.

---

85. this] *Q 2;* his *Q 1, Q 3.*   96. cares] *Q 2;* care *Q 1, Q 3.*
92. to] *Q 2;* for *Q 1, Q 3.*   101. repress] *Q 1–2;* expresse *Q 3.*

103–104. *fire . . . flame*] proverbial; see Tilley, F 265.

If Fates had taken you from earthly life
Before beginning of this civil strife,
Perhaps your sons in their unmastered youth,   110
Loose from regard of any living wight,
Would run on headlong with unbridled race
To their own death and ruin of this realm.
But sith the gods, that have the care for kings,
Of things and times, dispose the order so   115
That in your life this kindled flame breaks forth,
While yet your life, your wisdom, and your power
May stay the growing mischief and repress
The fiery blaze of their enkindled heat,
It seems, and so ye ought to deem thereof,   120
That loving Jove hath tempered so the time
Of this debate to happen in your days
That you yet living may the same appease
And add it to the glory of your age;
And they, your sons, may learn to live in peace.   125
Beware, O king, the greatest harm of all,
Lest by your wailful plaints your hastened death
Yield larger room unto their growing rage.
Preserve your life, the only hope of stay.
And if your highness herein list to use   130
Wisdom or force, counsel or knightly aid,
Lo we, our persons, powers, and lives are yours.
Use us till death, O king; we are your own.

EUBULUS.

Lo, here the peril that was erst foreseen
When you, O king, did first divide your land   135
And yield your present reign unto your sons.
But now, O noble prince, now is no time
To wail and plain and waste your woeful life.
Now is the time for present good advice.
Sorrow doth dark the judgment of the wit.   140

119. enkindled] *Q 1–2;* vnkindled   124. your age] *Dodsley;* your latter
Q 3.   age *Q 1–3.*
                                                                 125. your] *Q 3;* our *Q 1–2.*

___

122. *debate*] strife.

"The heart unbroken and the courage free
From feeble faintness of bootless despair
Doth either rise to safety or renown
By noble valor of unvanquished mind,
Or yet doth perish in more happy sort."   145
Your grace may send to either of your sons
Some one both wise and noble personage
Which, with good counsel and with weighty name
Of father, shall present before their eyes
Your hest, your life, your safety, and their own,   150
The present mischief of their deadly strife.
And in the while, assemble you the force
Which your commandment and the speedy haste
Of all my lords here present can prepare.
The terror of your mighty power shall stay   155
The rage of both, or yet of one at least.

[*Enter* Nuntius.]

NUNTIUS.

O king, the greatest grief that ever prince did hear,
That ever woeful messenger did tell,
That ever wretched land hath seen before,
I bring to you. Porrex, your younger son,   160
With sudden force invaded hath the land
That you to Ferrex did allot to rule;
And with his own most bloody hand he hath
His brother slain and doth possess his realm.

GORBODUC.

O heavens, send down the flames of your revenge!   165
Destroy, I say, with flash of wreakful fire
The traitor son and then the wretched sire!
But let us go, that yet perhaps I may
Die with revenge and 'pease the hateful gods.   [*Exeunt.*]

141–145.] There may be a proverbial basis for this sententious statement;
see Tilley, H 305.

142. *bootless*] remediless.

156.1. *Nuntius*] a messenger who, in the classical tradition, describes
action, usually violent, that has taken place offstage.

CHORUS.

The lust of kingdom knows no sacred faith,   170
　　No rule of reason, no regard of right,
No kindly love, no fear of heaven's wrath;
　　But with contempt of gods and man's despite,
Through bloody slaughter doth prepare the ways
　　To fatal scepter and accursed reign.   175
The son so loathes the father's lingering days,
　　Ne dreads his hand in brother's blood to stain.

O wretched prince, ne dost thou yet record
　　The yet fresh murders done within the land
Of thy forefathers, when the cruel sword   180
　　Bereft Morgan his life with cousin's hand?
Thus fatal plagues pursue the guilty race,
　　Whose murderous hand, imbrued with guiltless blood,
Asks vengeance still before the heaven's face
　　With endless mischiefs on the cursed brood.   185

The wicked child thus brings to woeful sire
　　The mournful plaints to waste his very life.
Thus do the cruel flames of civil fire
　　Destroy the parted reign with hateful strife.
And hence doth spring the well from which doth flow   190
　　The dead black streams of mourning, plaints, and woe.

The Order and Signification of the Dumb Show
Before the Fourth Act

First, the music of hautboys began to play, during which
there came forth from under the stage, as though out of hell,

---

170. kingdom] *Q 2;* kingdomes *Q 1,*
Q 3.
179. land] *Q 2;* lands *Q 1, Q 3.*
184. still] *Q 2; not in Q 1, Q 3.*
186. thus] *Q 2;* this *Q 1, Q 3.*

187. very] *Q 2;* wery *Q 1;* weary
Q 3.
191. mourning] *Q 2;* mournings
Q 1, Q 3.
[Dumb Show]
2. forth] *Q 1, Q 3; not in Q 2.*

---

　　1. *hautboys*] Oboes, woodwind instruments used as a treble to the bassoon,
have a thin, plaintive tone.

three Furies, Alecto, Megaera, and Tisiphone, clad in black
garments sprinkled with blood and flames, their bodies girt
with snakes, their heads spread with serpents instead of hair,　5
the one bearing in her hand a snake, the other a whip, and
the third a burning firebrand, each driving before them a
king and a queen which, moved by Furies, unnaturally had
slain their own children. The names of the kings and queens
were these: Tantalus, Medea, Athamas, Ino, Cambises,　10
Althea. After that the Furies and these had passed about the
stage thrice, they departed, and then the music ceased.
Hereby was signified the unnatural murders to follow; that
is to say, Porrex slain by his own mother, and of King
Gorboduc and Queen Videna, killed by their own subjects.　15

[IV.i]　　　　　　　[*Enter*] Videna.

VIDENA.

Why should I live and linger forth my time
In longer life to double my distress?
O me, most woeful wight, whom no mishap

---

3. *three Furies*] The Erinyes, "the goddesses of vengeance," are sometimes
called the Eumenides, "the kind ones," in hopes of placating them. As
agents of justice, they are completely lacking in mercy; see below, IV.ii.277–
280.

10–11. *Tantalus . . . Althea*] For Tantalus, see above II.i.16–17, note.
Medea, wife of Jason, killed their two sons after he deserted her. Athamas and
Ino were the foster parents of Dionysus, the child of Zeus and the ill-fated,
too curious Semele. For their protective care of Dionysus, the jealous Hera
laid a plague of madness upon them: Athamas imagined his elder son
Learchus was a deer and killed him; Ino leapt into the sea with the younger
son Melikertes (Fox). Cambises, king of Persia, killed the son of Praxaspes,
his counselor, in a drunken wager; his exploits are the subject of a bombastic
play by Thomas Preston written before 1569. Althea, or Althaia, the mother
of Meleager, was told at his birth that he would die as soon as a brand on
the hearth was consumed. To forestall his end, Althea extinguished the
brand and hid it in a chest. Many years later, after Meleager had killed a
wild boar, he quarreled with his uncles over the awarding of the skin.
In anger he killed them, and Althea avenged her brothers' deaths by taking
the brand out of the chest and burning it. Meleager's sudden death proved
the prophecy true (Fox).
[IV.i]

1–81.] Cf. the extensive monologues of Seneca's *Medea*, ll. 1–55 and his
Octavia, ll. 1–33; also Lady Macbeth's at I.v.41–55: "Come, you spirits . . ."
(Walsh).

Long ere this day could have bereaved hence.
Mought not these hands, by fortune or by fate,   5
Have pierced this breast and life with iron reft?
Or in this palace here, where I so long
Have spent my days, could not that happy hour
Once, once have happed in which these hugy frames
With death by fall might have oppressed me?   10
Or should not this most hard and cruel soil,
So oft where I have pressed my wretched steps,
Sometime had ruth of mine accursed life
To rend in twain and swallow me therein?
So had my bones possessed now in peace   15
Their happy grave within the closed ground,
And greedy worms had gnawn this pined heart
Without my feeling pain; so should not now
This living breast remain the ruthful tomb,
Wherein my heart yelden to death is graved;   20
Nor dreary thoughts, with pangs of pining grief,
My doleful mind had not afflicted thus.
O my beloved son! O my sweet child!
My dear Ferrex, my joy, my life's delight!
Is my beloved son, is my sweet child,   25
My dear Ferrex, my joy, my life's delight,
Murdered with cruel death? O hateful wretch!
O heinous traitor both to heaven and earth!
Thou, Porrex, thou this damned deed hast wrought;
Thou, Porrex, thou shalt dearly 'bye the same.   30

7. long] *Q 1, Q 3;* loug *Q 2.*
14. and] *Q 1, Q 2 (corrected), Q 3;*
not in Q 2 (uncorrected).
22. had] *Q 1–2;* hath *Q 3.*

25. beloved] *Q 2;* wel beloued *Q 1,*
Q 3.
30. 'bye] *Q 2;* abye *Q 1, Q 3.*

5. *Mought*] might.

7–10. *Or . . . me*] "Why could not this palace have fallen on me and brought death before this hour?"

13. *ruth*] pity.

17. *pined*] wasted, suffering.

20. *yelden*] yielded.

20. *graved*] buried.

26. *My . . . delight*] The line may be a compositorial repetition of line 24 just above.

30. *'bye*] atone for.

Traitor to kin and kind, to sire and me,
To thine own flesh, and traitor to thyself,
The gods on thee in hell shall wreak their wrath,
And here in earth this hand shall take revenge
On thee, Porrex, thou false and caitiff wight.   35
If after blood so eager were thy thirst
And murderous mind had so possessed thee,
If such hard heart of rock and stony flint
Lived in thy breast that nothing else could like
Thy cruel tyrant's thought but death and blood,   40
Wild savage beasts, mought not their slaughter serve
To feed thy greedy will, and in the midst
Of their entrails to stain thy deadly hands
With blood deserved and drink thereof thy fill?
Or if naught else but death and blood of man   45
Mought please thy lust, could none in Britain land,
Whose heart betorn out of his panting breast
With thine own hand, or work what death thou wouldst,
Suffice to make a sacrifice to 'pease
That deadly mind and murderous thought in thee,   50
But he who in the selfsame womb was wrapped,
Where thou in dismal hour receivedst life?
Or if needs, needs thy hand must slaughter make,
Moughtest thou not have reached a mortal wound,
And with thy sword have pierced this cursed womb   55
That the accursed Porrex brought to light,
And given me a just reward therefor?
So Ferrex yet sweet life mought have enjoyed,
And to his aged father comfort brought
With some young son in whom they both might live.   60
But whereunto waste I this ruthful speech,
To thee that hast thy brother's blood thus shed?

---

41. their] *Q2;* the *Q1, Q3.*   53. thy] *Q1–2;* this *Q3.*
47. panting] *Q2;* louying *Q1;*   53. must] *Q1–2;* might *Q3.*
louing *Q3;* living *Dodsley.*   56. the] *Q1–3;* thee *Dodsley.*
49. 'pease] *Q2;* appeaze *Q1;* ap-   58. yet] *Q2;* if *Q1, Q3;* his *Dodsley.*
peaze *Q3.*   62. hast] *Q1–2;* hath *Q3.*

35. *caitiff wight*] treacherous creature.
39. *like*] satisfy.

Shall I still think that from this womb thou sprung?
That I thee bare? Or take thee for my son?
No, traitor, no; I thee refuse for mine!   65
Murderer, I thee renounce; thou art not mine.
Never, O wretch, this womb conceived thee,
Nor never bode I painful throes for thee.
Changeling to me thou art, and not my child,
Nor to no wight that spark of pity knew.   70
Ruthless, unkind, monster of nature's work,
Thou never sucked the milk of woman's breast,
But from thy birth the cruel tiger's teats
Have nursed thee; nor yet of flesh and blood
Formed is thy heart, but of hard iron wrought;   75
And wild and desert woods bred thee to life.
But canst thou hope to 'scape my just revenge,
Or that these hands will not be wroke on thee?
Dost thou not know that Ferrex' mother lives,
That loved him more dearly than herself?   80
And doth she live and is not venged on thee?   [*Exit.*]

[IV.ii]   [*Enter*] Gorboduc [*and*] Arostus.

GORBODUC.

We marvel much whereto this lingering stay
Falls out so long. Porrex unto our court,
By order of our letters, is returned;
And Eubulus received from us by hest,
At his arrival here, to give him charge   5
Before our presence straight to make repair,
And yet we have no word whereof he stays.

74. thee] *Q 2; not in Q 1, Q 3.*   [IV.ii]
78. wroke] *Q 1–2; wrekte Q 3.*   4. by hest] *Q 1–3;* behest *Dodsley.*
                                7. have] *Q 1–2;* heare *Q 3.*

68. *bode*] endured, bore.
69. *Changeling*] a child secretly put in the place of another.
71–76. *Ruthless . . . life*] cf. Virgil *Aeneid* iv. 365–367 and Seneca *Hercules Oetaeus*, ll. 143–146 (Walsh).
78. *wroke*] avenged.
[IV.ii]
4. *by hest*] by command.
6. *make repair*] appear.

AROSTUS.

Lo where he comes, and Eubulus with him.

[*Enter* Eubulus *and* Porrex.]

EUBULUS.

According to your highness' hest to me,
Here have I Porrex brought, even in such sort   10
As from his wearied horse he did alight,
For that your grace did will such haste therein.

GORBODUC.

We like and praise this speedy will in you,
To work the thing that to your charge we gave.
Porrex, if we so far should swerve from kind   15
And from those bounds which law of nature sets
As thou hast done by vile and wretched deed
In cruel murder of thy brother's life,
Our present hand could stay no longer time,
But straight should bathe this blade in blood of thee   20
As just revenge of thy detested crime.
No; we should not offend the law of kind
If now this sword of ours did slay thee here;
For thou hast murdered him, whose heinous death
Even nature's force doth move us to revenge   25
By blood again; and justice forceth us
To measure death for death, thy due desert.
Yet since thou art our child, and sith as yet
In this hard case what word thou canst allege
For thy defense by us hath not been heard,   30
We are content to stay our will for that
Which justice bids us presently to work
And give thee leave to use thy speech at full,
If aught thou have to lay for thine excuse.

PORREX.

Neither, O king, I can or will deny   35
But that this hand from Ferrex life hath reft;

16. those] *Q 2;* these *Q 1, Q 3.*   28. since] *Sackville-West;* sithens
16. law] *Q 2;* lawes *Q 1, Q 3.*   *Q 1–3.*
26. and] *Q 2;* But *Q 1, Q 3.*

10. *sort*] condition.

Which fact how much my doleful heart doth wail,
O would it mought as full appear to sight
As inward grief doth pour it forth to me.
So yet, perhaps, if ever ruthful heart   40
Melting in tears within a manly breast,
Through deep repentance of his bloody fact,
If ever grief, if ever woeful man
Might move regret with sorrow of his fault,
I think the torment of my mournful case,   45
Known to your grace as I do feel the same,
Would force even Wrath herself to pity me.
But as the water troubled with the mud
Shows not the face which else the eye should see,
Even so your ireful mind with stirred thought   50
Cannot so perfectly discern my cause.
But this unhap, amongst so many heaps,
I must content me with, most wretched man,
That to myself I must reserve my woe
In pining thoughts of mine accursed fact,   55
Since I may not show here my smallest grief,
Such as it is and as my breast endures,
Which I esteem the greatest misery
Of all mishaps that fortune now can send.
Not that I rest in hope with plaint and tears   60
To purchase life; for to the gods I clepe
For true record of this my faithful speech;
Never this heart shall have the thoughtful dread
To die the death that by your grace's doom,
By just desert, shall be pronounced to me;   65
Nor never shall this tongue once spend the speech,
Pardon to crave or seek by suit to live.
I mean not this as though I were not touched

43. man] *Q 1–2;* men *Q 3.*   61. To] *Q 2;* Should *Q 1, Q 3.*
54. reserve] *Q 2;* referre *Q 1, Q 3.* 66. the] *Q 2;* this *Q 1, Q 3;* his
56. Since] *Q 2;* Sithens *Q 1;* Si- *Dodsley.*
thence *Q 3.*

48–49. *water . . . see*] proverbial; see Tilley, W 100.
52. *heaps*] i.e., heaps of unhaps; some modern editors read *haps.*
61. *clepe*] call.
64. *doom*] judgment.

With care of dreadful death or that I held
Life in contempt, but that I know the mind   70
Stoops to no dread, although the flesh be frail.
And for my guilt, I yield the same so great
As in myself I find a fear to sue
For grant of life.

GORBODUC.   In vain, O wretch, thou showest
A woeful heart; Ferrex now lies in grave,   75
Slain by thy hand.

PORREX.   Yet this, O father, hear;
And then I end. Your majesty well knows
That, when my brother Ferrex and myself
By your own hest were joined in governance
Of this your grace's realm of Britain land,   80
I never sought nor travailed for the same;
Nor by myself nor by no friend I wrought,
But from your highness' will alone it sprung,
Of your most gracious goodness bent to me.
But how my brother's heart even then repined   85
With swollen disdain against mine egal rule,
Seeing that realm, which by descent should grow
Wholly to him, allotted half to me;
Even in your highness' court he now remains,
And with my brother then in nearest place,   90
Who can record what proof thereof was showed
And how my brother's envious heart appeared?
Yet I that judged it my part to seek
His favor and good will, and loath to make
Your highness know the thing which should have brought   95
Grief to your grace and your offense to him,
Hoping my earnest suit should soon have won
A loving heart within a brother's breast,
Wrought in that sort that, for a pledge of love
And faithful heart, he gave to me his hand.   100
This made me think that he had banished quite
All rancor from his thought and bare to me
Such hearty love as I did owe to him.

82. nor by no] *Q2;* or by no *Q1,*   97. my] *Q2;* by *Q1, Q3.*
Q3.

But after once we left your grace's court
And from your highness' presence lived apart,   105
This egal rule still, still did grudge him so
That now those envious sparks, which erst lay raked
In living cinders of dissembling breast,
Kindled so far within his heart disdain
That longer could he not refrain from proof   110
Of secret practice to deprive me life
By poison's force; and had bereft me so,
If mine own servant, hired to this fact
And moved by truth with hate to work the same,
In time had not bewrayed it unto me.   115
When thus I saw the knot of love unknit,
All honest league and faithful promise broke,
The law of kind and truth thus rent in twain,
His heart on mischief set and in his breast
Black treason hid, then, then, did I despair   120
That ever time could win him friend to me;
Then saw I how he smiled with slaying knife
Wrapped under cloak; then saw I deep deceit
Lurk in his face and death prepared for me.
Even nature moved me then to hold my life   125
More dear to me than his and bade this hand,
Since by his life my death must needs ensue
And by his death my life to be preserved,
To shed his blood and seek my safety so.
And wisdom willed me without protract   130
In speedy wise to put the same in ure.
Thus have I told the cause that moved me
To work my brother's death; and so I yield
My life, my death, to judgment of your grace.

109. heart] *Q 2;* hartes *Q 1, Q 3.*   115. In] *Q 1–2;* If *Q 3.*
111. me] *Q 1–2;* my *Q 3.*

---

107. *raked*] covered.
110. *proof*] attempt.
115. *bewrayed*] revealed.
122–123. *Then . . . cloak*] "Obviously taken from Chaucer: 'Ther saugh
I . . ./ The smylere with the knyf under the cloke' (*Knight's Tale* 1998–9)"
(Herrick).
130. *protract*] delay.

GORBODUC.

    O cruel wight, should any cause prevail   135
    To make thee stain thy hands with brother's blood?
    But what of thee we will resolve to do
    Shall yet remain unknown. Thou in the mean
    Shalt from our royal presence banished be
    Until our princely pleasure further shall   140
    To thee be showed. Depart therefore our sight,
    Accursed child!   [*Exit* Porrex.]
            What cruel destiny,
    What froward fate hath sorted us this chance,
    That even in those where we should comfort find,
    Where our delight now in our aged days   145
    Should rest and be, even there our only grief
    And deepest sorrows to abridge our life,
    Most pining cares and deadly thoughts do grow?

AROSTUS.

    Your grace should now, in these grave years of yours,
    Have found ere this the price of mortal joys,   150
    How short they be, how fading here in earth,
    How full of change, how brittle our estate,
    Of nothing sure save only of the death
    To whom both man and all the world doth owe
    Their end at last; neither should nature's power   155
    In other sort against your heart prevail,
    Than as the naked hand whose stroke assays
    The armed breast where force doth light in vain.

GORBODUC.

    Many can yield right sage and grave advice
    Of patient sprite to others wrapped in woe   160
    And can in speech both rule and conquer kind,
    Who, if by proof they might feel nature's force

---

148. grow] *Q 2;* graue *Q 1, Q 3.*   159. sage and grave] *Q 2;* graue and
155. should] *Q 2;* shall *Q 1, Q 3.*   sage *Q 1, Q 3.*

---

   138. *mean*] meanwhile.
   143. *sorted*] decreed, allotted.
   149–155. *Your . . . last*] Herrick, conceding that such complaints about
the fickleness of Fortune are commonplace (see Tilley, J 90), finds a close
parallel in one of Seneca's *Moral Epistles*: "Everything is slippery, deceitful,
and more changeable than weather. Nothing is sure for anyone but death."

Would show themselves men as they are indeed,
Which now will needs be gods. But what doth mean
The sorry cheer of her that here doth come?   165

[*Enter* Marcella.]

MARCELLA.

O where is ruth, or where is pity now?
Whither is gentle heart and mercy fled?
Are they exiled out of our stony breasts,
Never to make return? Is all the world
Drowned in blood and sunk in cruelty?   170
If not in women mercy may be found,
If not, alas, within the mother's breast
To her own child, to her own flesh and blood,
If ruth be banished thence, if pity there
May have no place, if there no gentle heart   175
Do live and dwell, where should we seek it then?

GORBODUC.

Madam, alas, what means your woeful tale?

MARCELLA.

O silly woman I, why to this hour
Have kind and fortune thus deferred my breath
That I should live to see this doleful day?   180
Will ever wight believe that such hard heart
Could rest within the cruel mother's breast,
With her own hand to slay her only son?
But out, alas, these eyes beheld the same;
They saw the dreary sight and are become   185
Most ruthful records of the bloody fact.
Porrex, alas, is by his mother slain,
And with her hand, a woeful thing to tell,

165. of her] *Q 1–2; not in Q 3.*

---

165. *sorry cheer*] sorrowful countenance.
169–170. *Is . . . cruelty?*] Another probable Senecan parallel, this time
to *Hippolytus*, ll. 551–552 (Herrick).
178. *silly*] weak, feeble (*OED*).
179. *deferred*] prolonged.
185. *dreary*] horridly depressing, bloody.
186. *records*] witnesses.

While slumbering on his careful bed he rests,
His heart, stabbed in with knife, is reft of life. 190

GORBODUC.

O Eubulus, O draw this sword of ours
And pierce this heart with speed! O hateful light,
O loathsome life, O sweet and welcome death!
Dear Eubulus, work this, we thee beseech!

EUBULUS.

Patient your grace; perhaps he liveth yet, 195
With wound received, but not of certain death.

GORBODUC.

O let us then repair unto the place,
And see if Porrex live or thus be slain.

[*Exeunt* Gorboduc *and* Eubulus.]

MARCELLA.

Alas, he liveth not! It is too true
That with these eyes, of him a peerless prince, 200
Son to a king, and in the flower of youth,
Even with a twink a senseless stock I saw.

AROSTUS.

O damned deed!

MARCELLA.   But hear his ruthful end:
The noble prince, pierced with the sudden wound,
Out of his wretched slumber hastely start, 205
Whose strength now failing, straight he overthrew,
When in the fall his eyes, even new unclosed,
Beheld the queen and cried to her for help.
We then, alas, the ladies which that time
Did there attend, seeing that heinous deed, 210
And hearing him oft call the wretched name
Of mother and to cry to her for aid
Whose direful hand gave him the mortal wound,
Pitying, alas, for nought else could we do,

---

190. stabbed] *Q 2;* stalde *Q 1, Q 3.*
198. if] *Q 2;* if that *Q 1, Q 3.*
198. live] *Q 2; not in Q 1, Q 3.*

203. his] *Q 2;* this *Q 1, Q 3.*
204. wound] *Q 1–2;* wounds *Q 3.*
207. new] *Q 1–2;* nowe *Q 3.*

---

202. *with a twink*] in a twinkling.
205. *hastely start*] hastily started.
206. *overthrew*] fell down.

His ruthful end, ran to the woeful bed,   215
Despoiled straight his breast, and all we might,
Wiped in vain with napkins next at hand
The sudden streams of blood that flushed fast
Out of the gaping wound. O what a look,
O what a ruthful steadfast eye methought   220
He fixed upon my face, which to my death
Will never part fro me, when with a braid
A deep-fet sigh he gave, and therewithal
Clasping his hands, to heaven he cast his sight.
And straight, pale death pressing within his face,   225
The flying ghost his mortal corpse forsook.

AROSTUS.

Never did age bring forth so vile a fact.

MARCELLA.

O hard and cruel hap that thus assigned
Unto so worthy a wight so wretched end;
But most hard, cruel heart that could consent   230
To lend the hateful destinies that hand
By which, alas, so heinous crime was wrought.
O queen of adamant, O marble breast!
If not the favor of his comely face,
If not his princely cheer and countenance,   235
His valiant active arms, his manly breast,
If not his fair and seemly personage,
His noble limbs in such proportion cast
As would have wrapt a silly woman's thought;
If this mought not have moved thy bloody heart   240
And that most cruel hand the wretched weapon
Even to let fall and kissed him in the face,
With tears for ruth to reave such one by death,
Should nature yet consent to slay her son?
O mother, thou to murder thus thy child!   245

---

215. ruthful] *Q 1–2;* rufull *Q 3.*   240. thy] *Q 2;* the *Q 1, Q 3.*
238. proportion] *Q 2–3;* prepara-   242. kissed] kiste *Q 1–3;* kiss *Haw-*
cion *Q 1.*   *kins.*

---

216. *Despoiled straight*] uncovered quickly.
222. *braid*] start.
223. *deep-fet*] deep-fetched.

Even Jove with justice must with lightning flames
From heaven send down some strange revenge on thee.
Ah, noble prince, how oft have I beheld
Thee mounted on thy fierce and trampling steed,
Shining in armor bright before the tilt,   250
And with thy mistress' sleeve tied on thy helm,
And charge thy staff, to please thy lady's eye,
That bowed the head-piece of thy friendly foe!
How oft in arms on horse to bend the mace,
How oft in arms on foot to break the sword,   255
Which never now these eyes may see again!

AROSTUS.

Madam, alas, in vain these plaints are shed;
Rather with me depart and help to 'suage
The thoughtful griefs that in the aged king
Must needs by nature grow by death of this   260
His only son whom he did hold so dear.

MARCELLA.

What wight is that which saw that I did see
And could refrain to wail with plaint and tears?
Not I, alas! That heart is not in me.
But let us go, for I am grieved anew   265
To call to mind the wretched father's woe.   [*Exeunt.*]

CHORUS.

When greedy lust in royal seat to reign
    Hath reft all care of gods and eke of men;
And cruel heart, wrath, treason, and disdain,
    Within ambitious breast are lodged, then   270
Behold how mischief wide herself displays,
And with the brother's hand the brother slays.

When blood thus shed doth stain the heaven's face,
    Crying to Jove for vengeance of the deed,

---

258. 'suage] *Q 2;* asswage *Q 1, Q 3.*   *Q 3.*
270. Within] *Q 2;* Within the *Q 1,*   274. the] *Q 2;* this *Q 1, Q 3.*

248–256.] "The details, taken from medieval romance, are of course
anachronistic" (Walsh).
251. *sleeve*] token, favor.
252. *charge thy staff*] level thy lance.

The mighty god even moveth from his place   275
    With wrath to wreak. Then sends he forth with speed
The dreadful Furies, daughters of the night,
    With serpents girt, carrying the whip of ire,
With hair of stinging snakes, and shining bright
    With flames and blood, and with a brand of fire.   280
These, for revenge of wretched murder done,
Do make the mother kill her only son.

Blood asketh blood, and death must death requite;
    Jove, by his just and everlasting doom,
Justly hath ever so requited it.   285
    The times before record and times to come
Shall find it true, and so doth present proof
Present before our eyes for our behoof.

O happy wight that suffers not the snare
    Of murderous mind to tangle him in blood;   290
And happy he that can in time beware
    By other's harms and turn it to his good.
But woe to him that, fearing not to offend,
Doth serve his lust and will not see the end.

The Order and Signification of the Dumb Show
Before the Fifth Act

First, the drums and flutes began to sound, during which
there came forth upon the stage a company of harquebussiers and of armed men, all in order of battle. These,
after their pieces discharged, and that the armed men had
three times marched about the stage, departed, and then the   5
drums and flutes did cease. Hereby was signified tumults,

276. sends] *Q 1–2;* send *Q 3.*   286. The] *Q 2;* These *Q 1, Q 3;*
282. Do make] *Q 1–2;* Dooth cause   This *Dodsley.*
Q 3.

---

283. *Blood . . . blood*] proverbial; see Tilley, B 458.
291. *beware*] benefit.
[Dumb Show]
2–3. *harquebussiers*] men armed with harquebuses, an early portable gun,
fired by a matchlock and trigger and supported on a forked staff during
firing. "As the dumb shows were symbolic, not realistic, the use of firearms
need not be regarded as anachronistic" (Walsh).

rebellions, arms, and civil wars to follow as fell in the realm
of Great Britain which, by the space of fifty years and more,
continued in civil war between the nobility after the death
of King Gorboduc and of his issues, for want of certain   10
limitation in the succession of the crown, till the time of
Dunwallo Molmutius, who reduced the land to monarchy.

[V.i]   [*Enter*] Clotyn, Mandud, Gwenard, Fergus, [*and*] Eubulus.

CLOTYN.

    Did ever age bring forth sych tyrants' hearts?
    The brother hath bereft the brother's life;
    The mother, she hath dyed her cruel hands
    In blood of her own son; and now at last
    The people, lo, forgetting truth and love,   5
    Contemning quite both law and loyal heart,
    Even they have slain their sovereign lord and queen.

MANDUD.

    Shall this their traitorous crime unpunished rest?
    Even yet they cease not, carried on with rage
    In their rebellious routs, to threaten still   10
    A new bloodshed unto the prince's kin,
    To slay them all and to uproot the race
    Both of the king and queen; so are they moved
    With Porrex' death, wherein they falsely charge
    The guiltless king, without desert at all,   15
    And traitorously have murdered him therefor,
    And eke the queen.

GWENARD.   Shall subjects dare with force
    To work revenge upon their prince's fact?

[Dumb Show]   *Q 1.*
11. the succession] *Q 1, Q 3;* succes-   [V.i]
sion *Q 2.*   1. tyrants'] *Q 1–3;* tyrant *Dodsley.*
12. monarchy]   *Q 2–3;* Monarche   9. on] *Q 2;* out *Q 1, Q 3.*

---

  12. *Dunwallo Molmutius*] A son of Clotyn of Cornwall, he subjugated
the whole island and restored the realm to its former estate in his rule of
forty years (Geoffrey of Monmouth).
  12. *reduced the land*] brought the land under control.
[V.i]
  15. *desert*] the fact of deserving reward or punishment.

Admit the worst that may, as sure in this
The deed was foul, the queen to slay her son,   20
Shall yet the subject seek to take the sword,
Arise against his lord, and slay his king?
O wretched state, where those rebellious hearts
Are not rent out even from their living breasts,
And with the body thrown unto the fowls   25
As carrion food for terror of the rest.

FERGUS.

There can no punishment be thought too great
For this so grievous crime. Let speed therefore
Be used therein, for it behooveth so.

EUBULUS.

Ye all, my lords, I see consent in one,   30
And I as one consent with ye in all.
I hold it more than need, with sharpest law
To punish this tumultous bloody rage.
For nothing more may shake the common state
Than sufferance of uproars without redress;   35
Whereby how some kingdoms of mighty power,
After great conquests made, and flourishing
In fame and wealth, have been to ruin brought.
I pray to Jove that we may rather wail
Such hap in them than witness in ourselves.   40
Eke fully with the duke my mind agrees
That no cause serves whereby the subject may
Call to account the doings of his prince,
Much less in blood by sword to work revenge,
No more than may the hand cut off the head;   45
In act nor speech, no, not in secret thought
The subject may rebel against his lord
Or judge of him that sits in Caesar's seat,
With grudging mind to damn those he mislikes.
Though kings forget to govern as they ought,   50
Yet subjects must obey as they are bound.
But now, my lords, before ye farther wade,

32. with] *Q 2;* with the *Q 1, Q 3.*   42–49. That ... mislikes] *Q 1, Q 3;*
33. this] *Q 2;* the *Q 1, Q 3;* their   *not in Q 2.*
Dodsley.   49. to] *Dodsley;* do *Q 1, Q 3.*

Or spend your speech, what sharp revenge shall fall
By justice' plague on these rebellious wights,
Methinks ye rather should first search the way   55
By which in time the rage of this uproar
Mought be repressed and these great tumults ceased.
Even yet the life of Britain land doth hang
In traitors' balance of unegal weight.
Think not, my lords, the death of Goboduc,   60
Nor yet Videna's blood, will cease their rage.
Even our own lives, our wives and children dear,
Our country, dearest of all, in danger stands,
Now to be spoiled, now, now made desolate,
And by ourselves a conquest to ensue.   65
For give once sway unto the people's lusts
To rush forth on and stay them not in time,
And as the stream that rolleth down the hill
So will they headlong run with raging thoughts
From blood to blood, from mischief unto moe,   70
To ruin of the realm, themselves, and all,
So giddy are the common people's minds,
So glad of change, more wavering than the sea.
Ye see, my lords, what strength these rebels have,
What hugy number is assembled still;   75
For though the traitorous fact for which they rose
Be wrought and done, yet lodge they still in field;
So that how far their furies yet will stretch
Great cause we have to dread. That we may seek
By present battle to repress their power,   80
Speed must we use to levy force therefor;
For either they forthwith will mischief work
Or their rebellious roars forthwith will cease.
These violent things may have no lasting long.
Let us therefore use this for present help: 85
Persuade by gentle speech and offer grace

62. dear] *Q 2; not in Q 1, Q 3.*   84. long] *Q 2;* londe *Q 1, Q 3;*
83. will] *Q 1–2;* must *Q 3.*   stonde *Dodsley.*

72–73. So . . . sea] from *Hercules Furens,* l. 170 and from *Octavia,* ll. 877–
881 (Herrick). Sackville in *The Complaint* gives Buckingham a similar
sentiment (ll. 421–427) (Walsh).

With gift of pardon, save unto the chief;
And that upon condition that forthwith
They yield the captains of their enterprise
To bear such guerdon of their traitorous fact   90
As may be both due vengeance to themselves
And wholesome terror to posterity.
This shall, I think, scatter the greatest part
That now are holden with desire of home,
Wearied in field with cold of winter's nights,   95
And some, no doubt, stricken with dread of law.
When this is once proclaimed, it shall make
The captains to mistrust the multitude,
Whose safety bids them to betray their heads;
And so much more because the rascal routs   100
In things of great and perilous attempts
Are never trusty to the noble race.
And while we treat and stand on terms of grace,
We shall both stay their fury's rage the while
And eke gain time, whose only help sufficeth   105
Withouten war to vanquish rebels' power.
In the meanwhile, make you in readiness
Such band of horsemen as ye may prepare.
Horsemen, you know, are not the commons' strength,
But are the force and store of noble men,   110
Whereby the unchosen and unarmed sort
Of skilless rebels, whom none other power
But number makes to be of dreadful force,
With sudden brunt may quickly be oppressed.
And if this gentle mean of proffered grace   115
With stubborn hearts cannot so far avail
As to assuage their desperate courages,
Then do I wish such slaughter to be made
As present age and eke posterity
May be adrad with horror of revenge   120
That justly then shall on these rebels fall.
This is, my lords, the sum of mine advice.

93. scatter] Q 2; flatter Q 1, Q 3.   skillish Q 3.
112. skilless] Q 2; skillische Q 1;   122. lords] Q 1, Q 2; lord Q 2.

90. *guerdon*] recompense.

CLOTYN.

> Neither this case admits debate at large,
> And, though it did, this speech that hath been said
> Hath well abridged the tale I would have told.   125
> Fully with Eubulus do I consent
> In all that he hath said; and if the same
> To you, my lords, may seem for best advice,
> I wish that it should straight be put in ure.

MANDUD.

> My lords, then let us presently depart   130
> And follow this that liketh us so well.

> > [*Exeunt* Clotyn, Mandud, Gwenard, *and* Eubulus.]

FERGUS.

> If ever time to gain a kingdom here
> Were offered man, now it is offered me.
> The realm is reft both of their king and queen;
> The offspring of the prince is slain and dead;   135
> No issue now remains, the heir unknown;
> The people are in arms and mutinies;
> The nobles, they are busied how to cease
> These great rebellious tumults and uproars;
> And Britain land, now desert, left alone   140
> Amid these broils, uncertain where to rest,
> Offers herself unto that noble heart
> That will or dare pursue to bear her crown.
> Shall I, that am the Duke of Albany,
> Descended from that line of noble blood   145
> Which hath so long flourished in worthy fame
> Of valiant hearts, such as in noble breasts
> Of right should rest above the baser sort,
> Refuse to venture life to win a crown?
> Whom shall I find enemies that will withstand   150
> My fact herein, if I attempt by arms

148. the] *Q 1, Q 3;* the the *Q 2.*   149. venture] *Q 2;* aduenture *Q 1, Q 3.*

---

126. *consent*] agree.
130. *presently*] immediately.
131. *liketh*] pleaseth.
144.] According to Geoffrey, Albany was the last of five kings who held out against Dunwallo.

To seek the same now in these times of broil?
These dukes' power can hardly well appease
The people that already are in arms.
But if perhaps my force be once in field,   155
Is not my strength in power above the best
Of all these lords now left in Britain land?
And though they should match me with power of men,
Yet doubtful is the chance of battles joined.
If victors of the field we may depart,   160
Ours is the scepter then of Great Britain;
If slain amid the plain this body lie,
Mine enemies yet shall not deny me this,
But that I died giving the noble charge
To hazard life for conquest of a crown.   165
Forthwith, therefore, will I in post depart
To Albany and raise in armor there
All power I can; and here my secret friends
By secret practice shall solicit still
To seek to win to me the people's hearts.   [*Exit.*] 170

[V.ii]   [*Enter*] Eubulus.

EUBULUS.

O Jove, how are these people's hearts abused!
What blind fury thus headlong carries them!
That though so many books, so many rolls
Of ancient time, record what grievous plagues
Light on these rebels aye, and though so oft   5
Their ears have heard their aged fathers tell
What just reward these traitors still receive,
Yea, though themselves have seen deep death and blood,
By strangling cord and slaughter of the sword
To such assigned, yet can they not beware,   10

152. same] *Q 2;* Fame *Q 1, Q 3.*   [V.ii]
162. lie] *Q 2;* be *Q 1, Q 3.*   4. time] *Q 1–2;* time of *Q 3.*

---

167. *Albany*] his kingdom, Albania or Scotland.
[V.ii]
3. *rolls*] historical accounts.

Yet cannot stay their lewd rebellious hands;
But suffering, lo, foul treason to distain
Their wretched minds, forget their loyal heart,
Reject all truth, and rise against their prince.
A ruthful case, that those whom duty's bond,   15
Whom grafted law by nature, truth, and faith
Bound to preserve their country and their king,
Born to defend their commonwealth and prince,
Even they should give consent thus to subvert
Thee, Britain land, and from thy womb should spring,   20
O native soil, those that will needs destroy
And ruin thee and eke themselves in fine.
For lo, when once the dukes had offered grace
Of pardon sweet, the multitude, misled
By traitorous fraud of their ungracious heads,   25
One sort that saw the dangerous success
Of stubborn standing in rebellious war
And knew the difference of prince's power
From headless number of tumultuous routs,
Whom common country's care and private fear   30
Taught to repent the error of their rage,
Laid hands upon the captains of their band
And brought them bound unto the mighty dukes.
And other sort, not trusting yet so well
The truth of pardon, or mistrusting more   35
Their own offense than that they could conceive
Such hope of pardon for so foul misdeed,
Or for that they their captains could not yield,

11. cannot] *Q 2;* can they not *Q 1,*   20. spring] *Q 2;* bring *Q 1, Q 3.*
Q 3.   23. dukes] *Q 2;* Duke *Q 1, Q 3.*
11. lewd] *Q 2; not in Q 1, Q 3.*   31. error] *Q 2;* terror *Q 1, Q 3.*
12. lo] *Q 2;* to *Q 1;* too *Q 3.*   34. And other] *Q 2;* An other *Q 1;*
15. bond] *Q 2;* bounde *Q 1;* bound   Another *Q 3.*
Q 3.   36. could] *Q 2;* should *Q 1, Q 3.*
20. thy] *Q 2;* the *Q 1, Q 3.*

11. *lewd*] base.
12. *distain*] dishonor.
22. *in fine*] finally.
25. *fraud . . . heads*] deceiving their unsophisticated discriminations.
26. *One sort*] one part.

Who, fearing to be yielded, fled before,
Stale home by silence of the secret night.   40
The third unhappy and enraged sort
Of desperate hearts who, stained in princes' blood,
From traitorous furor could not be withdrawn
By love, by law, by grace, ne yet by fear,
By proffered life, ne yet by threatened death,   45
With minds hopeless of life, dreadless of death,
Careless of country and aweless of God,
Stood bent to fight, as Furies did them move,
With violent death to close their traitorous life.
These all by power of horsemen were oppressed   50
And with revenging sword slain in the field
Or with the strangling cord hanged on the trees,
Where yet their carrion carcasses do preach
The fruits that rebels reap of their uproars
And of the murder of their sacred prince.   55
But lo, where do approach the noble dukes
By whom these tumults have been thus appeased.

[*Enter* Clotyn, Mandud, Gwenard, *and* Arostus.]

CLOTYN.

I think the world will now at length beware
And fear to put on arms against their prince.

MANDUD.

If not, those traitorous hearts that dare rebel,   60
Let them behold the wide and hugy fields
With blood and bodies spread of rebels slain,
The lofty trees clothed with the corpses dead
That, strangled with the cord, do hang thereon.

---

41. enraged] Q2; vnraged Q1, Q3.   62. of] Q2; with Q1, Q3.
52. trees] Q1, Q3; tree Q2.   63. lofty] Q2; lustie Q1, Q3.
53. their] Q2; the Q1, Q3.   63. the] Q2; not in Q1, Q3.
53. preach] Q2; proache Q1, Q3.   64. thereon] Q2; therin Q1; there-
60. dare] Q1–2; do Q3.   in Q3.
62. bodies] Q2; bodie Q1, Q3.

---

40. *Stale*] stole.
50. *oppressed*] overwhelmed.

AROSTUS.

    A just reward; such as all times before   65
    Have ever lotted to those wretched folks.

GWENARD.

    But what means he that cometh here so fast?

             [*Enter* Nuntius.]

NUNTIUS.

    My lords, as duty and my troth doth move
    And of my country work a care in me,
    That, if the spending of my breath availed   70
    To do the service that my heart desires,
    I would not shun to embrace a present death;
    So have I now, in that wherein I thought
    My travail mought perform some good effect,
    Ventured my life to bring these tidings here.   75
    Fergus, the mighty duke of Albany,
    Is now in arms and lodgeth in the field
    With twenty thousand men. Hither he bends
    His speedy march and minds to invade the crown.
    Daily he gathereth strength and spreads abroad   80
    That to this realm no certain heir remains,
    That Britain land is left without a guide,
    That he the scepter seeks for nothing else
    But to preserve the people and the land,
    Which now remain as ship without a stern.   85
    Lo, this is that which I have here to say.   [*Exit* Nuntius.]

CLOTYN.

    Is this his faith? and shall he falsely thus
    Abuse the vantage of unhappy times?
    O wretched land, if his outrageous pride,
    His cruel and untempered wilfulness,   90
    His deep dissembling shows of false pretense,

---

69. work a] *Q 2;* work and *Q 1, Q 3;*   86. here to say] *Q 2;* hereto saide
worken *Dodsley.*   *Q 1;* hereto said *Q 3;* hereto sain
70. availed] *Q 2;* auaile *Q 1, Q 3.*   *Dodsley.*

---

   66. *lotted*] allotted.

   85. *stern*] "The steering gear of a ship, the rudder and the helm together,
but often applied to the rudder only" (*OED*).

Should once attain the crown of Britain land!
Let us, my lords, with timely force resist
The new attempt of this our common foe
As we would quench the flames of common fire.   95

MANDUD.

Though we remain without a certain prince
To weld the realm or guide the wandering rule,
Yet now the common mother of us all,
Our native land, our country, that contains
Our wives, children, kindred, ourselves, and all   100
That ever is or may be dear to man,
Cries unto us to help ourselves and her.
Let us advance our powers to repress
This growing foe of all our liberties.

GWENARD.

Yea, let us so, my lords, with hasty speed.   105
And ye, O gods, send us the welcome death,
To shed our blood in field, and leave us not
In loathsome life to linger out our days
To see the hugy heaps of these unhaps
That now roll down upon the wretched land,   110
Where empty place of princely governance,
No certain stay now left of doubtless heir,
Thus leave this guideless realm an open prey
To endless storms and waste of civil war.

AROSTUS.

That ye, my lords, do so agree in one,   115
To save your country from the violent reign
And wrongfully usurped tyranny
Of him that threatens conquest of you all,
To save your realm, and in this realm yourselves,
From foreign thraldom of so proud a prince,   120
Much do I praise; and I beseech the gods
With happy honor to requite it you.
But, O my lords, sith now the heaven's wrath
Hath reft this land the issue of their prince,
Sith of the body of our late sovereign lord   125

108. days] *Q 2;* lyues *Q 1;* liues *Q 3.*   122. honor] *Q 1–3;* howers *Dodsley.*
109. unhaps] *Q 1–2;* mishaps *Q 3.*

Remains no moe since the young kings be slain,
And of the title of descended crown
Uncertainly the divers minds do think,
Even of the learned sort, and more uncertainly
Will partial fancy and affection deem,   130
But most uncertainly will climbing pride
And hope of reign withdraw to sundry parts
The doubtful right and hopeful lust to reign.
When once this noble service is achieved
For Britain land, the mother of ye all,   135
When once ye have with armed force repressed
The proud attempts of this Albanian prince
That threatens thraldom to your native land,
When ye shall vanquishers return from field
And find the princely state an open prey   140
To greedy lust and to usurping power,
Then, then, my lords if ever kindly care
Of ancient honor of your ancestors,
Of present wealth and noblesse of your stocks,
Yea, of the lives and safety yet to come   145
Of your dear wives, your children, and yourselves,
Might move your noble hearts with gentle ruth,
Then, then, have pity on the torn estate;
Then help to salve the well-near hopeless sore;
Which ye shall do if ye yourselves withhold   150
The slaying knife from your own mother's throat;
Her shall you save, and you, and yours in her
If ye shall all with one assent forbear
Once to lay hand or take unto yourselves
The crown, by color of pretended right,   155
Or by what other means so ever it be,
Till first by common counsel of you all
In parliament the regal diadem

127. of descended] *Q 2;* of the   132. to] *Q 2;* from *Q 1, Q 3.*
discended *Q 1, Q 3.*

---

130. *partial*] biased.
133. *lust*] overmastering desire.
137. *Albanian*] of Albanact, i.e., Scotland.
144. *noblesse*] nobility.
155. *color*] pretense.

Be set in certain place of governance;
In which your parliament, and in your choice,   160
Prefer the right, my lords, without respect
Of strength or friends, or whatsoever cause
That may set forward any other's part.
For right will last, and wrong cannot endure.
Right mean I his or hers upon whose name   165
The people rest by mean of native line,
Or by the virtue of some former law,
Already made their title to advance.
Such one, my lords, let be your chosen king,
Such one so born within your native land;   170
Such one prefer; and in no wise admit
The heavy yoke of foreign governance.
Let foreign titles yield to public wealth.
And with that heart wherewith ye now prepare
Thus to withstand the proud invading foe,   175
With that same heart, my lords, keep out also
Unnatural thraldom of stranger's reign;
Ne suffer you, against the rules of kind,
Your mother land to serve a foreign prince.

EUBULUS.

Lo, here the end of Brutus' royal line,   180
And lo, the entry to the woeful wreck
And utter ruin of this noble realm.
The royal king and eke his sons are slain;
No ruler rests within the regal seat;
The heir, to whom the scepter 'longs, unknown;   185
That to each force of foreign princes' power,
Whom vantage of our wretched state may move

161. without] *Q 1, Q 3;* with *Q 2.*   187. our] *Q 2;* your *Q 1, Q 3.*
162. or friends] *Q 2;* of frends *Q 1,*   187. may move] *Q 2; not in Q 1, Q 3;*
Q 3.   may tempt *Dodsley.*
186. each] *Q 1–2;* the *Q 3.*

160. *parliament*] an evident anachronism but one that reveals the bias
of the play.
165. *his or hers*] L. H. Courtney (*Notes & Queries,* Second Series, X [1860],
261–263) interprets the phrase as a covert argument for the justice of the
claim of Lady Catherine Grey.
173. *wealth*] well-being.
177. *stranger*] foreigner.

By sudden arms to gain so rich a realm,
And to the proud and greedy mind at home
Whom blinded lust to reign leads to aspire,   190
Lo, Britain realm is left an open prey,
A present spoil by conquest to ensue.
Who seeth not now how many rising minds
Do feed their thoughts with hope to reach a realm?
And who will not by force attempt to win   195
So great a gain, that hope persuades to have?
A simple color shall for title serve.
Who wins the royal crown will want no right,
Nor such as shall display by long descent
A lineal race to prove him lawful king.   200
In the meanwhile these civil arms shall rage,
And thus a thousand mischiefs shall unfold,
And far and near spread thee, O Britain land!
All right and law shall cease, and he that had
Nothing today tomorrow shall enjoy   205
Great heaps of gold, and he that flowed in wealth,
Lo, he shall be bereft of life and all;
And happiest he that then possesseth least.
The wives shall suffer rape, the maids deflowered;
And children fatherless shall weep and wail;   210
With fire and sword thy native folk shall perish;
One kinsman shall bereave another's life;
The father shall unwitting slay the son;
The son shall slay the sire and know it not.
Women and maids the cruel soldier's sword   215
Shall pierce to death, and silly children, lo,
That playing in the streets and fields are found,
By violent hands shall close their latter day.
Whom shall the fierce and bloody soldier
Reserve to life? Whom shall he spare from death?   220
Even thou, O wretched mother, half alive,

200. lawful] Q 2; selfe a Q 1, Q 3.   212. another's] Q 2; an other Q 1,
206. gold] Q 2; good Q 1, Q 3.   Q 3.
207. bereft] Q 2; reft Q 1, Q 3.   217. playing] Q 1, Q 3; play Q 2.

203. spread] spread over.
216. silly] defenseless, innocent.

Thou shalt behold thy dear and only child
Slain with the sword while he yet sucks thy breast.
Lo, guiltless blood shall thus each where be shed.
Thus shall the wasted soil yield forth no fruit,   225
But dearth and famine shall possess the land.
The towns shall be consumed and burnt with fire,
The peopled cities shall wax desolate;
And thou, O Britain, whilom in renown,
Whilom in wealth and fame, shalt thus be torn,   230
Dismembered thus, and thus be rent in twain,
Thus wasted and defaced, spoiled and destroyed.
These be the fruits your civil wars will bring.
Hereto it comes when kings will not consent
To grave advice, but follow wilful will.   235
This is the end when in fond princes' hearts
Flattery prevails and sage rede hath no place.
These are the plagues, when murder is the mean
To make new heirs unto the royal crown.
Thus wreak the gods when that the mother's wrath   240
Naught but the blood of her own child may 'suage;
These mischiefs spring when rebels will arise
To work revenge and judge their prince's fact.
This, this ensues when noble men do fail
In loyal troth, and subjects will be kings.   245
And this doth grow, when lo, unto the prince
Whom death or sudden hap of life bereaves,
No certain heir remains, such certain heir,
As not all-only is the rightful heir,
But to the realm is so made known to be,   250
And troth thereby vested in subjects' hearts
To owe faith there where right is known to rest.

---

227. burnt] *Q2–3;* brent *Q1.*
229. Britain] *Q2; Brittaine* Land
Q1, Q3.
236. fond] *Q2;* yonge *Q1;* yong
Q3.
242. spring] *Q2;* springs *Q1;*

springes *Q3.*
248. such certain heir] *Q2;* suche
certentie *Q1, Q3.*
250. known] *Q2;* vnknowen *Q1;*
vnknowne *Q3.*

---

229. *whilom*] once.
237. *rede*] advice.
249. *all-only*] solely.

Alas, in parliament what hope can be,
When is of parliament no hope at all,
Which, though it be assembled by consent,   255
Yet is not likely with consent to end;
While each one for himself, or for his friend,
Against his foe shall travail what he may;
While now the state, left open to the man
That shall with greatest force invade the same,   260
Shall fill ambitious minds with gaping hope;
When will they once with yielding hearts agree?
Or in the while, how shall the realm be used?
No, no; then parliament should have been holden,
And certain heirs appointed to the crown,   265
To stay the title of established right
And in the people plant obedience
While yet the prince did live whose name and power
By lawful summons and authority
Might make a parliament to be of force   270
And might have set the state in quiet stay.
But now, O happy man whom speedy death
Deprives of life, ne is enforced to see
These hugy mischiefs and these miseries,
These civil wars, these murders, and these wrongs   275
Of justice. Yet must God in fine restore
This noble crown unto the lawful heir;
For right will always live and rise at length,
But wrong can never take deep root to last.   [*Exeunt.*]

The end of the tragedy of King Gorboduc.

256. is] *Q 2;* is it *Q 1, Q 3.*
266. the] *Q 2;* their *Q 1, Q 3.*
267. in the people plant] *Q 2;* plant
the people in *Q 1, Q 3.*
271. state] *Q 1–2;* Realme *Q 3.*

272. whom] *Q 1–2;* what *Q 3;* that
Dodsley.
276. God] *Q 2;* Ioue *Q 1, Q 3.*
279.1. *The . . . Gorboduc*] *Q 1, Q 3;*
not in *Q 2.*

264–271. *No . . . stay*] a bald statement of the political purpose of the
play.
278. *right . . . length*] proverbial; see Tilley, T 579.

Appendix A

The Reply of Elizabeth to the House of Commons Touching the Succession

As I have good cause, so do I give you all my hearty thanks for the good zeal and loving care you seem to have, as well towards me as to the whole state of your country. Your petition, I perceive, consisteth of three parts, and mine answer to the same shall depend of two.

And to the first part, I may say unto you that from my years of understanding, sith I first had consideration of myself to be born a servitor of Almighty God, I happily chose this kind of life in which I yet live, which I assure you for mine own part hath hitherto best contented myself and I trust hath been most acceptable to God. From the which, if either ambition of high estate offered to me in marriage by the pleasure and appointment of my prince—whereof I have some records in this presence, as you our Lord Treasurer well know; or if the eschewing of the danger of mine enemies or the avoiding of the peril of death, whose messenger or rather continual watchman, the prince's indignation, was not little time daily before mine eyes—by whose means, although I know or justly may suspect, yet I will not now utter; or if the whole cause were in my sister herself, I will not now burthen her therewith, because I will not charge the dead: if any of these, I say, could have drawn or dissuaded me from this kind of life, I had not now remained in this estate wherein you see me. But so constant have I always continued in this determination—although my youth and words may seem to some hardly to agree together—yet is it most true that at this day I stand free from any other meaning that either I have had in times past or have at this present. With which trade of life I am so thoroughly acquainted that I trust God, who hath hitherto therein preserved and led me by the hand, will not now of His goodness suffer me to go alone.

For the other part, the manner of your petition I do well like of and take in good part, because that it is simple and containeth no limitation of place or person. If it had been otherwise, I must needs have misliked it very much and thought it in you a great presumption, being unfitting and altogether unmeet for you to require them that may command, or those to appoint whose parts are to desire, or such to bind and limit whose duties are to obey, or to take upon you to draw my love to your liking or frame my will to your fantasies; for a guerdon constrained and a gift freely given can never agree together. Nevertheless—if any of you be in suspect—whensoever it may please God to incline my heart to another kind of life, ye may well assure yourselves my meaning is not to do or determine anything wherewith the realm may or shall have just cause to be discontented. And therefore put that clean out of your heads. For I assure you— what credit my assurance may have with you I cannot tell, but what credit it shall deserve to have the sequence shall declare—I will never in that matter conclude anything that shall be prejudicial to the realm, for the weal, good, and safety whereof I will never shun to spend my life. And whomsoever my chance shall be to light upon, I trust he shall be as careful for the realm and you—I will not say as myself, because I cannot so certainly determine of any other; but at the least ways, by my good will and desire he shall be such as shall be as careful for the preservation of the realm and you as myself.

And albeit it might please Almighty God to continue me still in this mind to live out of the state of marriage, yet it is not to be feared but He will so work in my heart and in your wisdoms as good provision by His help may be made in convenient time, whereby the realm shall not remain destitute of an heir that may be a fit governor, and peradventure more beneficial to the realm than such offspring as may come of me. For, although I be never so careful of your well doings and mind ever so to be, yet may my issue grow out of kind and become perhaps ungracious. And in the end, this shall be for me sufficient, that a marble stone shall declare that a Queen, having reigned such a time, lived and died a virgin.

And here I end, and take your coming unto me in good part, and give unto you all eftsoons my hearty thanks, more yet for your zeal and good meaning than for your petition.

Appendix B

Chronology

Approximate years are indicated by *, occurrences in doubt by (?).

Political and Literary Events	Life and Major Works of Sackville and Norton
1532	Norton born in Bedfordshire.
1536	Sackville born at Buckhurst, Sussex.
1544	Norton admitted to Cambridge.
1550	Norton translates and publishes a Latin letter by Peter Martyr to the Duke of Somerset.
1551	Sackville in residence at Oxford,* Cambridge (?). Some commendatory verses by Norton published in *Turner's Preservative*, an anti-Pelagian tract.
1553	Sackville settles in London.
1555	Sackville marries Cecily Baker of Kent, daughter of a Privy Councilor; admitted to the Inner Temple. Norton admitted to the Inner Temple; marries Margery, daughter of Archbishop Cramner.
1557	Norton publishes his *Epitaph of Henry Williams* in Tottel's collection of *Songs and Sonnets*.

1558

Accession of Queen Elizabeth I.
Robert Greene born.
Thomas Kyd born.

Sackville elected to Parliament for Westmoreland, Norton for Gatton.

1560

George Chapman born.

Jasper Heywood commends Sackville's poems and Norton's "ditties."

1561

Francis Bacon born.

Sackville's commendatory verses to Sir Thomas Hoby's *Courtier*, a translation of Castiglione's *Il Cortegiano*.
Norton publishes his translation of Calvin's *Institutions* (later editions in 1562, 1574, 1587, 1599) and contributes metrical versions of twenty-eight psalms to Sternhold and Hopkins' collection.

1562

First performance of *GORBODUC*, January 6; repeated by royal command, January 18.
Norton elected to Parliament for Berwick; becomes standing counsel to the Stationers' Company.

1563

Sackville's *Induction and Complaint of the Duke of Buckingham* appear in *A Mirror for Magistrates*; on foreign tour in France and Italy.
Norton a member of the Parliamentary Commission appointed to consider the limitation of succession, recommending the Queen's marriage.

1564

Shakespeare born.
Christopher Marlowe born.

1565

Norton enters Pembroke Hall, Oxford; M.A. 1569.
Sackville returns home.

1567

Sackville knighted, raised to the peerage as Lord Buckhurst, June 8. Norton marries, after his first wife's death, her cousin, Alice Cramner; begins publishing many controversial tracts against the Roman Catholic Church.

1568

Sackville sent on official visit to France; persuades the Queen Mother to make "a motion for the marriage of Elizabeth with her second son, the Duke of Anjou."

1569

Sackville in office as joint Lord Lieutenant of Sussex.*

1570

Norton translates and publishes Nowell's *Catechism*.

1571

Sackville's second official visit to France to congratulate Charles IX on his marriage; returned with Paul do Foix to continue the discussion of Elizabeth's marriage; created M.A., Cambridge.
Norton appointed "Remembrancer" to the Lord Mayor of London; elected M.P. for London.

1572
Thomas Dekker born.*
John Donne born.
Massacre of St. Bartholomew's Day.

Sackville a member of the Privy Council; employed as commissioner at state trials.

1573
Ben Jonson born.*

1574
Thomas Heywood born.*

1576
The Theatre, the first permanent public theater in London, established by James Burbage.
John Marston born.

1577
The Curtain theater opened.
Holinshed's *Chronicles of England, Scotland and Ireland*.
Drake begins circumnavigation of the earth; completed 1580.

1578
John Lyly's *Euphues: The Anatomy of Wit*.

1579
John Fletcher born.
Sir Thomas North's translation of Plutarch's *Lives*.

Norton travels to Rome to seek information about Catholics.

1580
Thomas Middleton born.

Norton sent to Guernsey to investigate complaints about the Governor.

1581

Norton becomes official censor of the Queen's Catholic subjects; appointed by Bishop of London as licenser of the press; one of the commissioners at the trial of Edmund Campion.

1582

Norton complains to Walsingham of the nickname "Rackmaster General" given to him for his part in torturing Catholics; confined to his house some of the year because of his extremism.

1583
Philip Massinger born.

Norton a member of a commission to examine affairs in Sark.

1584
Francis Beaumont born.*

Norton confined to the Tower for his open dissatisfaction with the episcopal establishment; released through Walsingham's influence; dies in his house at Sharpenhoe, Bedfordshire, March 10.

1586

Death of Sir Philip Sidney.
John Ford born.
Kyd's *THE SPANISH TRAGEDY*.

Sackville announces the death sentence to Mary Stuart.

1587

The Rose theater opened by Henslowe.
Marlowe's *TAMBURLAINE*, Part I.*
Execution of Mary, Queen of Scots.
Drake raids Cadiz.

Sackville sent to examine affairs in the Low Countries and particularly Leicester's conduct; recalled, placed under house arrest for too closely following Elizabeth's instructions.

1588

Defeat of the Spanish Armada.
Marlowe's *TAMBURLAINE*, Part II.*

Sackville appointed commissioner for ecclesiastical causes.

1589

Greene's *FRIAR BACON AND FRIAR BUNGAY*.*
Marlowe's *THE JEW OF MALTA*.*

Sackville elected Knight of the Garter, April 24; in November on an embassy to the Low Countries.

1590

Spenser's *Faerie Queene* (Books I–III) published.
Sidney's *Arcadia* published.
Shakespeare's *HENRY VI*, Parts I–III,* *TITUS ANDRONICUS*.*

1591

Shakespeare's *RICHARD III*.*

Sackville signs treaty with France on behalf of Elizabeth; elected Chancellor of Oxford.

1592

Marlowe's *DOCTOR FAUSTUS** and *EDWARD II*.*
Shakespeare's *TAMING OF THE SHREW** and *THE COMEDY OF ERRORS*.*
Death of Greene.

Sackville incorporated M.A., Oxford; receives Queen on her visit there.

1593

Shakespeare's *LOVE'S LABOR'S LOST*;* *Venus and Adonis* published.
Death of Marlowe.
Theaters closed on account of plague.

1594

Shakespeare's *TWO GENTLEMEN OF VERONA;** *The Rape of Lucrece* published.
Shakespeare's company becomes Lord Chamberlain's Men.
Death of Kyd.

1595

The Swan theater built.
Sidney's *Defense of Poesy* published.
Shakespeare's *ROMEO AND JULIET,** *A MIDSUMMER NIGHT'S DREAM,** *RICHARD II.**
Raleigh's first expedition to Guiana.

1596

Spenser's *Faerie Queene* (Books IV–VI) published.
Shakespeare's *MERCHANT OF VENICE,** *KING JOHN.**
James Shirley born.

1597

Bacon's *Essays* (first edition).
Shakespeare's *HENRY IV*, Part I.*

1598

Demolition of The Theatre.
Shakespeare's *MUCH ADO ABOUT NOTHING,** *HENRY IV*, Part II.*
Jonson's *EVERY MAN IN HIS HUMOR* (first version).
Seven books of Chapman's translation of Homer's *Iliad* published.

Sackville joins Burghley unsuccessfully to negotiate peace with Spain; goes abroad for last time to renew a treaty with the united provinces.

1599

The Paul's Boys reopen their theater.
The Globe theater opened.
Shakespeare's *AS YOU LIKE IT,** *HENRY V*, *JULIUS CAESAR.**
Marston's *ANTONIO AND MELLIDA,** Parts I and II.
Dekker's *THE SHOEMAKERS' HOLIDAY.**
Death of Spenser.

Sackville installed as Lord Treasurer, succeeding Burghley.

1600

Shakespeare's *TWELFTH NIGHT.**
The Fortune theater built by Alleyn.
The Children of the Chapel begin to play at the Blackfriars.

1601

Shakespeare's *HAMLET,** *MERRY WIVES OF WINDSOR.**
Insurrection and execution of the Earl of Essex.
Jonson's *POETASTER.*

Sackville appointed Lord High Steward; later to preside at trials of Essex and his fellow conspirators.

1602

Shakespeare's *TROILUS AND CRESSIDA.**

1603

Death of Queen Elizabeth I; accession of James VI of Scotland as James I.
Florio's translation of Montaigne's *Essays* published.
Shakespeare's *ALL'S WELL THAT ENDS WELL.**
Heywood's *A WOMAN KILLED WITH KINDNESS.*
Marston's *THE MALCONTENT.**
Shakespeare's company becomes the King's Men.

Sackville appointed by King James as Lord Treasurer for life, November; sits as peer in judgment of Lords Cobham and Grey.

1604

Shakespeare's *MEASURE FOR MEASURE,** *OTHELLO.**
Marston's *THE FAWN.**
Chapman's *BUSSY D'AMBOIS.**

Sackville created Earl of Dorset, March 13; negotiates new treaty with Spain, signed in August; receives pension of £1,000 from the King of Spain.

1605

Shakespeare's *KING LEAR.**
Marston's *THE DUTCH COURTESAN.**
Bacon's *Advancement of Learning* published.
The Gunpowder Plot.

Sackville entertains King James at Oxford.

1606
Shakespeare's *MACBETH.**
Jonson's *VOLPONE.**
Tourneur's *REVENGER'S TRAG-
EDY.**
The Red Bull theater built.
Death of John Lyly.

1607
Shakespeare's *ANTONY AND
CLEOPATRA.**
Beaumont's *KNIGHT OF THE
BURNING PESTLE.**
Settlement of Jamestown, Virginia.

1608
Shakespeare's *CORIOLANUS,**
*TIMON OF ATHENS,** *PERI-
CLES.**
Chapman's *CONSPIRACY AND
TRAGEDY OF CHARLES, DUKE
OF BYRON.**
Richard Burbage leases Blackfriars
theater for King's company.
John Milton born.

Sackville dies suddenly at council
table in Whitehall, April 19.

1609
Shakespeare's *CYMBELINE;**
Sonnets published.
Jonson's *EPICOENE.*
Dekker's *Gull's Hornbook* published.

1610
Jonson's *ALCHEMIST.*
Chapman's *REVENGE OF BUSSY
D'AMBOIS.**
Richard Crashaw born.

1611
Authorized (King James) Version
of the Bible published.
Shakespeare's *THE WINTER'S
TALE,** *THE TEMPEST.**
Beaumont and Fletcher's *A KING
AND NO KING.*
Middleton's *A CHASTE MAID IN
CHEAPSIDE.**

Tourneur's *ATHEIST'S TRAG-EDY.**

Chapman's translation of *Iliad* completed.

1612

Webster's *THE WHITE DEVIL.**

1613

The Globe theater burned.

Shakespeare's *HENRY VIII* (with Fletcher).

Webster's *THE DUCHESS OF MALFI.**

Sir Thomas Overbury murdered.

1614

The Globe theater rebuilt.

The Hope theater built.

Jonson's *BARTHOLOMEW FAIR.*

1616

Publication of Folio edition of Jonson's *Works*.

Chapman's *Whole Works of Homer.*

Death of Shakespeare.

Death of Beaumont.

1618

Outbreak of Thirty Years War.

Execution of Raleigh.

1620

Settlement of Plymouth, Massachusetts.

1621

Middleton's *WOMEN BEWARE WOMEN.**

Robert Burton's *Anatomy of Melancholy* published.

Andrew Marvell born.

1622

Middleton and Rowley's *THE CHANGELING.**

Henry Vaughan born.

1623

Publication of Folio edition of Shakespeare's *COMEDIES, HISTORIES, AND TRAGEDIES.*

1625
Death of King James I; accession of
Charles I.
Death of Fletcher.

1626
Death of Tourneur.
Death of Bacon.

1627
Death of Middleton.

1628
Ford's *THE LOVER'S MELAN-
CHOLY*.
Petition of Right.
Buckingham assassinated.

1631
Shirley's *THE TRAITOR*.
Death of Donne.
John Dryden born.

1632
Massinger's *THE CITY MADAM*.*

1633
Donne's *Poems* published.
Death of George Herbert.

1634
Death of Chapman, Marston, Web-
ster.*
Publication of *THE TWO NOBLE
KINSMEN*, with title-page attribu-
tion to Shakespeare and Fletcher.
Milton's *Comus*.

1635
Sir Thomas Browne's *Religio Medici*.

1637
Death of Jonson.

1639
First Bishops' War.
Death of Carew.*

1640
Short Parliament.
Long Parliament impeaches Laud.
Death of Massinger, Burton.

1641
Irish rebel.
Death of Heywood.

1642
Charles I leaves London; Civil War breaks out.
Shirley's *COURT SECRET.*
All theaters closed by Act of Parliament.

1643
Parliament swears to the Solemn League and Covenant.

1645
Ordinance for New Model Army enacted.

1646
End of First Civil War.

1647
Army occupies London.
Charles I forms alliance with Scots.
Publication of Folio edition of Beaumont and Fletcher's *COMEDIES AND TRAGEDIES.*

1648
Second Civil War.

1649
Execution of Charles I.

1650
Jeremy Collier born.

1651
Hobbes' *Leviathan* published.

1652
First Dutch War begins (ended 1654).
Thomas Otway born.

1653
Nathaniel Lee born.*

1656
D'Avenant's *THE SIEGE OF RHODES* performed at Rutland House.

1657

John Dennis born.

1658

Death of Oliver Cromwell.

D'Avenant's *THE CRUELTY OF THE SPANIARDS IN PERU* performed at the Cockpit.

1660

Restoration of Charles II.

Theatrical patents granted to Thomas Killigrew and Sir William D'Avenant, authorizing them to form, respectively, the King's and the Duke of York's Companies.

1661

Cowley's *THE CUTTER OF COLEMAN STREET*.

D'Avenant's *THE SIEGE OF RHODES* (expanded to two parts).

1662

Charter granted to the Royal Society.

1663

Dryden's *THE WILD GALLANT*.

Tuke's *THE ADVENTURES OF FIVE HOURS*.

1664

Sir John Vanbrugh born.

Dryden's *THE RIVAL LADIES*.

Dryden and Howard's *THE INDIAN QUEEN*.

Etherege's *THE COMICAL REVENGE*.

1665

Second Dutch War begins (ended 1667).

Great Plague.

Dryden's *THE INDIAN EMPEROR*.

Orrery's *MUSTAPHA*.

1666

Fire of London.

Death of James Shirley.